Lee and His Generals
The Ultimate Trivia Book

Wendy Sauers

BURD STREET PRESS

This Burd Street Press publication
was printed by
Beidel Printing House, Inc.
63 West Burd Street
Shippensburg, PA 17257-0152 USA

In respect for the scholarship contained herein, the acid-free paper used in this book meets the guidelines for permanence and durability of the Committee on Production Guidelines for Book Longevity of the Council on Library Resources.

For a complete list of available publications
please write
Burd Street Press
Division of White Mane Publishing Company, Inc.
P.O. Box 152
Shippensburg, PA 17257-0152 USA

Library of Congress Cataloging-in-Publication Data

Sauers, Wendy.
    Lee and his generals : the ultimate trivia book / Wendy Sauers.
       p. cm.
    Includes bibliographical references.
    ISBN 1-57249-196-5 (alk. paper)
    1. Generals--Confederate States of America--Miscellanea. 2. Lee, Robert E. (Robert Edward), 1807-1870--Miscellanea. 3. United States--History--Civil War, 1861-1865--Miscellanea. I. Title.

E467 .S26 2000
973.7'3'0922--dc21
                                                                    00-029780

PRINTED IN THE UNITED STATES OF AMERICA

In Memory of
Paul Bowersox
June 29, 1975–April 15, 1997

Contents

⚑Firsts

1. Who was the first officer of the old army to offer his sword and his life to North Carolina?
2. Who was the first officer to be wounded during the war?
3. What was Thomas Jackson's first duty during the war?
4. Who won the first engagement of the war?
5. Who received the first battlefield promotion of the war?
6. Who was the first former United States officer to offer his services to Virginia?
7. What was Jeb Stuart's first service during the war?
8. When was the first time that Robert E. Lee commanded troops?
9. Who was offered the honor of firing the first shot of the war?
10. What battle was Jackson's first battle as an independent commander?
11. What was Jubal Early's first assignment?
12. Who was the first civilian soldier to get a division command in the Army of Northern Virginia?
13. What was Robert E. Lee's first failure?
14. Who was the first and only soldier of Polish descent to become a Confederate general?
15. Where was James Longstreet's first combat experience?
16. What battle was Robert E. Lee's first victory?
17. When was A.P. Hill first defeated by a Union force?
18. What was Robert E. Lee's first official post?
19. When was the first time that Jackson drew his sword during the war?
20. What battle was James Longstreet's first combat as a division commander?
21. What battle was the first collaboration between Lee and Jackson?
22. What was the first engagement that Richard Ewell fought on his own?
23. What was the first battle lost by Lee as commander of the Army of Northern Virginia?
24. In what battle did Robert E. Lee first order the erection of field fortifications?
25. Whose division was the first to cross the Mason-Dixon Line during the Gettysburg campaign?
26. Whose brigade was the only brigade to end the war as an organized unit?
27. Who was the first brigade commander to be captured by the enemy after Robert E. Lee took command?

⬥Firsts (answers)

1. George Anderson.
2. Richard Ewell. He was wounded on June 1, 1861, during a skirmish at Fairfax Court House.
3. Commander at Harpers Ferry.
4. Daniel H. Hill on June 10, 1861, at Big Bethel, Virginia.
5. Arnold Elzey. He was promoted from colonel to brigadier general on July 21, 1861.
6. John Pegram on May 10, 1861.
7. He was under Thomas Jackson at Harpers Ferry.
8. In April 1855 when he took command of the Second Cavalry in Texas.
9. Roger Pryor. He turned it down.
10. Battle of Kernstown.
11. To train the volunteers who were gathering in Lynchburg.
12. William Taliaferro.
13. Cheat Mountain.
14. Zebulon York.
15. At Resaca de la Palma and Palo Alto during the Mexican War.
16. Battle of Gaines' Mill.
17. Bristoe Station on October 14, 1863.
18. Commander of the defenses of Virginia.
19. Battle of Cedar Mountain.
20. Battle of Williamsburg.
21. Battle of Second Manassas.
22. Battle of Cross Keys.
23. Battle of Mechanicsville on June 26, 1862.
24. Battle of Chancellorsville.
25. Robert Rodes'.
26. John Bratton's.
27. James Archer. He was captured at Gettysburg.

28. Who was the first and only general to swear in front of Robert E. Lee?
29. What was the first and only Confederate unit to be named for a person?
30. Who is the only American general ever to lose a war?
31. Under whom was Isaac Trimble's first line command?
32. What was Henry Heth's first battle with the Army of Virginia?
33. On June 23, 1862, Robert E. Lee held his first meeting with his generals. Who was present?
34. What was Richard Ewell's first order when he arrived at Chambersburg, Pennsylvania in June 1863?
35. Who has the honor of being the first Confederate to enter Gettysburg on July 1, 1863?
36. When was the army first addressed as "the Army of Northern Virginia"?
37. Who was the first elected governor of Mississippi after the war?
38. Who was the first commander of the Robert E. Lee Camp No. 1, United Confederate Veterans?
39. Who became the first president of Mississippi State College?
40. On whose casket did the first Confederate flag made drape?
41. Who was the first president of the Southern Historical Society?
42. Who was the first commander in chief of the United Confederate Veterans?
43. Who was the first president of the South Carolina Agricultural Society?

28. Jubal Early.
29. The Stonewall Brigade.
30. Robert E. Lee.
31. Richard Ewell.
32. Battle of Mechanicsville.
33. James Longstreet, Daniel H. Hill, Ambrose P. Hill, and Stonewall Jackson.
34. He forbade the sale of intoxicants, and he required that all who had them to report that they had them so a guard could be placed.
35. Abner Perrin and the First South Carolina.
36. On June 2, 1862. It was that day that Robert E. Lee took command.
37. Benjamin Humphreys.
38. John Rogers Cooke.
39. Stephen Lee.
40. Stonewall Jackson.
41. Jubal Early.
42. John Gordon.
43. Johnson Hagood.

♜West Point

1. Who supposedly introduced the song "Dixie" at the academy?
2. Whose future general's mother gave him a ham bone for good luck when he left home to attend West Point?
3. Who broke a plate over the head of Jubal Early?
4. Which future general, while on his way to the academy, stopped to visit Monticello?
5. While at West Point who once put rubber soles on his shoes so he could sneak into a different room and steal a pipe belonging to another cadet?
6. Who was dismissed in 1846 for failing mathematics?
7. Who contracted gonorrhea while on a summer furlough in 1844?
8. Who graduated first in his class in 1854?
9. Who was the last West Point general to die during the war?
10. Who graduated last in the class of 1847?
11. Who had no demerits while at West Point?
12. What was the rank of George Pickett when he graduated?
13. Who was the youngest graduate to rise to the rank of major general?
14. Instead of graduating in 1861 who went south and joined the Washington Artillery in New Orleans?
15. Who dropped his last name while at West Point?
16. Who was George McClellan's roommate?
17. Which future general was dismissed for pranks pulled on Christmas Eve in 1826?
18. Who studied the campaigns of Napoleon while he was superintendent at West Point?
19. Who was appointed superintendent in 1852?
20. Who secured Henry Heth's appointment to the academy?

✎West Point (answers)

1. James Dearing.
2. Ambrose P. Hill. He carried this with him for the rest of his life.
3. Lewis Armistead.
4. Jeb Stuart. He left with a chip of Thomas Jefferson's tombstone.
5. Cadmus Wilcox.
6. Birkett Fry.
7. Ambrose P. Hill.
8. George Washington Custis Lee. He graduated a rank higher than his father had.
9. Ambrose P. Hill.
10. Henry Heth.
11. Robert E. Lee.
12. Last.
13. Stephen Dodson Ramseur. He was 26 at the time.
14. Thomas Rosser.
15. Arnold Elzey Jones.
16. Ambrose P. Hill.
17. Benjamin Humphreys.
18. Robert E. Lee.
19. Robert E. Lee.
20. President John Tyler.

⚑Family

1. Which two of Robert E. Lee's ancestors signed the Declaration of Independence?
2. How was Brigadier General Samuel Garland, Jr. related to Louise Longstreet, the wife of James Longstreet?
3. Which general was the son-in-law of Governor Francis Pickens of South Carolina?
4. Who named his daughter Virginia Pelham?
5. Which general had 11 children in 11 years of marriage?
6. Lafayette McLaws was a nephew by marriage to which president?
7. At whose wedding was John Hunt Morgan the best man?
8. Which naval heroes was Matthew C. Butler related to?
9. Which general was the grandson of "Light-Horse" Harry Lee, and the great-grandson of George Mason?
10. Who was the brother-in-law of Alexander Lawton?
11. What was Phillip St. George Cooke Stuart's name changed to?
12. Whose aide-de-camp was Keith Armistead?
13. Which general was Robert E. Lee's military secretary, and also the son-in-law of Union General Edwin Sumner?
14. Who was Thomas F. Drayton's brother?
15. Whom did Rufus Barringer marry?
16. Who was a cousin of Henry Heth?
17. Whom was James Longstreet's mother related to by marriage?
18. Which general dropped his last name while at West Point?
19. To whom was John Esten Cooke related?
20. Who named his son Robert Lee?
21. Who married a sister of Edward Porter Alexander?
22. Who had a daughter born on October 17, 1862, the day after he had died?
23. Which general was a collateral descendant of President James Madison?
24. Who was Dudley DuBose's father-in-law?
25. Whom did Jeb Stuart marry?
26. Who was the brother-in-law of Jeb Stuart, and the son of Union General Philip St. George Cooke?
27. Who was Henry Wise's brother-in-law?
28. Who had as his uncle President Jefferson Davis?
29. Who was Martin Gary's brother-in-law?
30. Jubal Early was once heard to wish that the Federals would capture which general's wife?
31. Who married a sister of General John H. Morgan, and was also a brother-in-law of General Basil Duke?

✎Family (answers)

1. Richard Henry Lee and Francis Lightfoot Lee.
2. They were cousins.
3. Matthew Butler.
4. Jeb Stuart.
5. John Bell Hood.
6. Zachary Taylor.
7. Ambrose P. Hill. He also became his brother-in-law by marrying Kitty Grosh Morgan McClung.
8. He was a nephew of the Union naval heroes Oliver Hazard and Matthew C. Perry.
9. Fitzhugh Lee.
10. Edward Porter Alexander.
11. James Ewell Brown Stuart, Jr. This was due to his grandfather's, General Philip St. George Cooke, staying in the Union army.
12. Lewis Armistead. Keith was his son.
13. Armistead Long.
14. Captain Percival Drayton, who was in charge of the U.S.S. *Pocahontas.*
15. Eugenia Morrison, the sister of the wives of Thomas Jackson and Daniel H. Hill.
16. George Pickett.
17. Ulysses S. Grant.
18. Arnold Elzey Jones. For the rest of his life he used his paternal grandmother's maiden name.
19. He was the cousin of Flora Cooke Stuart, who was the wife of Jeb Stuart.
20. James Longstreet.
21. Alexander Lawton.
22. George Anderson.
23. Samuel Garland, Jr.
24. Robert Toombs.
25. Flora Cooke, the daughter of Union General Philip St. George Cooke.
26. John Cooke.
27. Union Major General George Gordon Meade.
28. Joseph Davis.
29. Nathan G. Evans.
30. Fanny Gordon, the wife of John Gordon. She went with him on all his campaigns.
31. A.P. Hill.

Profession

1. Who became a general in the army of Emperor Maximilian of Mexico?
2. Who represented Mississippi in the House of Representatives at the start of the war?
3. What was Robert E. Rodes' job prior to the war?
4. Who helped build the most famous route into the Shenandoah Valley?
5. Who resigned from the army to operate three iron factories?
6. Before the Mexican War which future general ran a pro-slavery newspaper?
7. Who held the office of rector of All Saints Church in Frederick, Maryland?
8. At the start of the war what was Thomas Jackson doing?
9. Who was the first president of the Southern Historical Society?
10. Where was Daniel H. Hill superintendent at the start of the war?
11. Who was once the Commonwealth's Attorney of Franklin County, Virginia?
12. Which general later served as governor of Virginia and as general in the Spanish-American War?
13. Who held the post of professor of engineering at the Virginia Military Institute?
14. Who led the force that went to Harpers Ferry to capture John Brown in 1859?
15. Who spent the remainder of his life as an insurance agent in Richmond?
16. What did Joseph Anderson buy in 1848?
17. After the war who served as doorkeeper of the United States House of Representatives?
18. At the war's beginning who was president and superintendent of the Norfolk and Petersburg Railroad?
19. Who was the youngest man ever elected vice-president of the United States?
20. Who once sat on the state supreme court in Georgia?
21. Who managed the Louisiana Lottery after the war?
22. Who in civilian life had collected extra post office payments for his mail coach business?
23. Who was secretary of the treasury under James Buchanan?

✎Profession (answers)

1. John Magruder.
2. William Barksdale.
3. Professor of engineering at the Virginia Military Institute.
4. Joseph Reid Anderson. The route was the Shenandoah Valley Turnpike.
5. Gustavus Woodson Smith.
6. William Barksdale.
7. William Pendleton.
8. Professor at the Virginia Military Institute.
9. Jubal Early.
10. North Carolina Military Institute.
11. Jubal Early.
12. Fitzhugh Lee.
13. Robert Rodes.
14. Captain Robert E. Lee.
15. George Pickett.
16. Tredegar Iron Company in Richmond.
17. Charles Field.
18. William Mahone.
19. John C. Breckinridge at the age of 35.
20. Henry Benning.
21. Jubal Early.
22. William Smith.
23. Howell Cobb.

⚑Religion

1. Who decided in 1863 that if he survived the war he would enter the ministry?
2. Whose funeral was conducted by the same rector who had married him?
3. Who made teamsters of the Dunkards who would not fight?
4. Who read the Episcopal burial service at Robert E. Lee's funeral?
5. Who was the Northern-born Quaker who became a Confederate general?
6. Who named his four cannon Matthew, Mark, Luke, and John?
7. Who was one of two ordained ministers who became Confederate generals?
8. Of what religion were Daniel H. Hill and Stephen Ramseur?
9. What did Richard Ewell and Robert E. Lee have in common?
10. What were Robert E. Lee's guiding principles?
11. What was George Pickett's favorite hymn?
12. Who became rector of Grace Church in 1853, a post he held until his death in 1883?
13. What hymn did Jeb Stuart ask to have sung as he lay dying?
14. Who read Psalm 118:17, "I shall not die, but live." What did he think it meant?

Religion (answers)

1. Clement Evans. In 1866 he began a career as a Methodist minister.
2. John Pegram. He was married on January 19, 1865. He died on February 5, 1865.
3. Stonewall Jackson.
4. William Pendleton.
5. Bushrod Johnson.
6. William Pendleton.
7. William Pendleton. Leonidas Polk was the other.
8. Presbyterian.
9. Both belonged to the Episcopal Church.
10. Duty and religion.
11. "Guide Me, O Thou Great Jehovah."
12. William Pendleton.
13. "Rock of Ages."
14. John Bell Hood. He took this to mean that he would survive the war.

⚑Nicknames

Match the nickname to the general in the right-hand column.

1. "Old Buck"
2. "Aunt Polly" or "Old Bob"
3. "Mudwall"
4. "Knight of the Golden Spurs"
5. "Old Swet"
6. "Old Polly"
7. "King of Spades"
8. "Little General"
9. "Old Reliable"
10. "Bull"
11. "Tiger John"
12. "Young Napoleon of the Railways"
13. "Rum"
14. "Old Gabe"
15. "Rooney"
16. "Grumble"
17. "Bald Eagle of Edgefield"
18. "Ranse"
19. "Old Rock"
20. "Old Jube" or "Old Jubilee"
21. "The Little Major"
22. "Extra Billy"
23. "Old Bull Dog"
24. "Old Bald Head"
25. "Noble Old Soldier"
26. "Shanks"
27. "Prince John"
28. "Old Blue Light" or "Old Jack"
29. "Old Allegheny"
30. "Tige" or "Tiger"
31. "Parlez"
32. "Little Powell"
33. "Hero of the Crater"
34. "My Old Warhorse"
35. "My bad old man"
36. "Old Pete"
37. "The eyes of this army"
38. "Fightin' Dick"
39. "Stonewall"
40. "Bull of the Woods"
41. "Beauty"

a. John Bratton
b. Winfield Featherston
c. John Jones
d. James Lane
e. William H.F. Lee
f. William Jackson
g. Jubal Early
h. John McCausland
i. Ambrose Wright
j. James Walker
k. William Terry
l. Edward Johnson
m. Raleigh Colston
n. Nathan Evans
o. Gabriel Wharton
p. Robert E. Lee
q. Ambrose P. Hill
r. Elisha Paxton
s. Richard Ewell
t. Jerome Robertson
u. Martin W. Gary
v. William Smith
w. Edward Porter Alexander
x. George Anderson
y. James Longstreet
z. John Magruder
aa. Jeb Stuart
bb. William Jones
cc. Thomas Jackson
dd. Henry Benning
ee. David Weisiger
ff. Richard Anderson

✎ Nicknames (answers)

1. k
2. t
3. f
4. aa
5. b
6. m
7. p
8. d
9. a
10. r
11. h
12. w
13. c
14. o
15. e
16. bb
17. u
18. i
19. dd
20. g
21. d
22. v
23. j
24. s
25. p
26. n
27. z
28. cc
29. l
30. x
31. m
32. q
33. ee
34. y
35. g
36. y
37. aa
38. ff
39. cc
40. y
41. aa

🏇 Horses

1. Which horse was temporarily lost when Stonewall Jackson entered Maryland in 1862?
2. Whose horse was named Rifle?
3. At Spotsylvania which horse reared just in time for a cannonball to pass under his belly?
4. How many horses did A.P. Hill have shot from under him during Second Bull Run?
5. Who had his bridle rein cut by a bullet during the battle of Gettysburg?
6. Was Traveller ever injured during the war?
7. Fourteen horses were hit in the volley that wounded which general?
8. During the Battle of Antietam which general's horse had his forelegs severed by a Federal shell?
9. To whom did the horse Nellie Gray belong?
10. Which general had seven horses shot from under him by the end of the war?
11. Which Union general had a horse named Breckinridge?
12. Who was severely injured a few days before Chancellorsville when his horse fell on him?
13. Which three generals rode a horse during Pickett's Charge?
14. Who owned a horse named Prince?
15. Where is Traveller buried?
16. During the Battle of Cross Keys a projectile wounded which general's horse?
17. Which horse did Ambrose P. Hill acquire after the Battle of Cedar Mountain?
18. Why did Richard Garnett ride his horse during Pickett's Charge?
19. What were the names of Robert E. Lee's five horses?
20. Which general fell from his horse shortly before he entered Maryland?
21. Where was the largest cavalry engagement of the war fought?
22. On May 12, 1864, which general had three horses shot from under him?
23. Who had a horse named Hero?
24. Who had three horses shot from under him during Antietam?
25. During the Battle of Second Manassas what did Richard Ewell usually do every time a horse was killed?
26. What were the names of Jeb Stuart's four horses?
27. After the Battle of Groveton which general had to be strapped into the saddle?
28. Shortly after Gettysburg what was Richard Ewell seen riding?

❦Horses (answers)

1. Little Sorrel.
2. Richard Ewell's.
3. Traveller.
4. Three.
5. Cadmus Wilcox.
6. No.
7. Stonewall Jackson.
8. Daniel H. Hill's.
9. Fitzhugh Lee. The horse was killed at Opequon.
10. Bryan Grimes.
11. Phil Sheridan. The horse had once belonged to John C. Breckinridge.
12. Cullen Battle.
13. Eppa Hunton, James Kemper, and Richard Garnett.
14. Ambrose P. Hill.
15. Just outside the chapel at Washington and Lee University in Lexington, Virginia.
16. Arnold Elzey's. Later during the same battle a rifle ball would kill it.
17. Champ, a gray stallion.
18. Earlier he had been kicked by his horse.
19. Traveller, Richmond, Brown-Roan, Lucy Long, and Ajax.
20. Stonewall Jackson.
21. Brandy Station.
22. Stephen Ramseur.
23. James Longstreet.
24. Daniel H. Hill.
25. He had the harness removed and sent to the rear.
26. Virginia, Highfly, Maryland, and Skylark.
27. Richard Ewell.
28. A mule.

♫Clothing

1. What did the citizens of Lynchburg give to John McCausland in 1864?
2. Which general had a beard so long he could tuck it under his belt?
3. Which general commanded in his shirt sleeves?
4. Who wore a straw hat during the third day at Gettysburg?
5. Whose sword was found in a pawnshop in Baltimore?
6. Who wore an ostrich feather in his hat?
7. At the Battle of First Bull Run who wore uniforms of the Union army?
8. Who dressed Stonewall Jackson for burial?
9. Which general liked to wear blue jeans, a hickory shirt, and a home-spun coat?
10. On September 19, 1861, A.P. Hill was given a flag from his wife. What was it made from?
11. Who used a scimitar instead of a sword?
12. Whose beard hid a receding chin?
13. What hat did John Gordon prefer instead of the kepi?
14. Who made A.P. Hill's calico and checkered shirts?
15. Who liked to wear a scarlet-lined cape fastened with a yellow sash?
16. Who carried his grandfather's Revolutionary War sword during the war?
17. Who so rarely used his sword that it rusted in the scabbard?
18. What was a trademark of A.P. Hill?
19. Who once captured the hat, military cloak, frock coat, and dispatch book and letters of Union General John Pope?
20. To whom were the belongings of the answer to Question 19 sent?
21. What did a group of women from Maryland once send to Robert E. Lee?
22. What was Stonewall Jackson wearing when he was buried?
23. Who bought a bolt of velveteen while in Chambersburg, Pennsylvania?
24. What type of hat did Robert E. Lee wear during the Gettysburg campaign?
25. What did Jeb Stuart wear in his hat?
26. What did Robert E. Lee give to William Roberts when he was commissioned a brigadier general?
27. To whom did Stonewall Jackson give the gold braid off his forage cap?
28. Who was accustomed to wearing a large white slouch hat that was topped off with a black plume?
29. Which general often wore a beaver hat?

✎ Clothing (answers)

1. A cavalry officer's uniform, a sword, spurs, and a horse.
2. Albert Jenkins.
3. Ambrose P. Hill. He rarely wore a uniform.
4. Cadmus Wilcox.
5. Richard Garnett.
6. Jeb Stuart.
7. Joseph Johnston, Pierre G.T. Beauregard, and James Longstreet.
8. Alexander Pendleton.
9. William E. Jones.
10. Material from her wedding dress.
11. Maxcy Gregg.
12. Jeb Stuart's.
13. Slouch hat.
14. His wife.
15. Jeb Stuart.
16. Richard Ewell.
17. Stonewall Jackson.
18. A black felt hat, and a red shirt.
19. Jeb Stuart.
20. Governor John Letcher.
21. A coat of gray English broadcloth.
22. Civilian clothes. This was because his uniform had been cut and blood-stained.
23. Gilbert Moxley Sorrel. He had a suit made from this bolt. He wore this uniform the remainder of the war.
24. A black felt hat.
25. A small Confederate flag which a lady in Columbia, South Carolina had asked him to wear.
26. His own gauntlets.
27. Janie Corbin. He gave it to her to twine in her hair as a remembrance. She would die of scarlet fever.
28. Jubal Early.
29. William Smith.

30. Before the Battle of Fredericksburg whom did Jeb Stuart give a new uniform coat?
31. Whose sword was hid in a privy when Major General David Hunter entered Lexington?
32. During the Verdiersville Raid what did Jeb Stuart lose?
33. Whose only indication of his rank were the three unwreathed stars on the collar of his coat?
34. What was Stonewall Jackson wearing when he first appeared in battle?
35. What did Jeb Stuart's wife make to keep his throat warm?
36. Whose wife made a necklace and bracelets from locks of her husband's hair?
37. During battle who wore a red turban and a red sash around his waist and shoulders?

30. Stonewall Jackson.
31. Stonewall Jackson. It was hidden by Mrs. Margaret Junkin Preston, his sister-in-law.
32. His plumed hat and cloak.
33. Robert E. Lee's.
34. The uniform of a professor of the Virginia Military Institute.
35. A fur collar.
36. Joseph Kershaw's wife.
37. Paul Semmes.

♌Money

1. Which general was reimbursed $200 for the loss of his horse Maggie?
2. What did Jeb Stuart bet to Samuel Crawford that the Federals would claim Cedar Mountain a Union victory?
3. How much did the government pay James Walker for the loss of his horse at Antietam?
4. How much was Robert E. Lee's yearly salary as president of Washington College?
5. How much did John Bell Hood's men give him so he could buy an artificial limb?
6. When John McCausland led his raid on Chambersburg, Pennsylvania what did he demand of the inhabitants?
7. For what invention was Jeb Stuart paid $5,000?
8. When William Wofford's mare was lost during the Battle of Cedarville what was its estimated value?
9. Which general wore a French-made cork leg that cost him $5,000?
10. What was the value of the 86 slaves owned by Goode Bryan?
11. Whom did Ambrose P. Hill's men give $10,000?
12. From whom did Ambrose Burnside once borrow $8,000?
13. For how much did Jeb Stuart have his life insured in early 1862?
14. Whom did Stonewall Jackson's headquarters staff give $800?
15. When Union General Phil Kearny was killed, his widow applied for his mount and horse supplies. Who had them appraised, paid for them, and sent them to her?
16. When John McCausland gave his list of demands to the citizens of Hagerstown, how did they react?
17. After the Battle of Port Republic who gave the wounded soldiers money out of his own pocket to aid them in their captivity?
18. On his invasion into Maryland how much money did Jubal Early levy on Hagerstown and Frederick?
19. Which general's memoirs were published to benefit the 10 children he left behind after his death?
20. Who is the only dead general to be pictured on Confederate currency?

⬣ Money (answers)

1. Richard Ewell. His horse had been shot from under him during the Battle of Gaines' Mill.
2. A hat.
3. $350.
4. $1,500.
5. $5,000.
6. He demanded $100,000 in gold or $500,000 in cash. When refused, more than four hundred buildings were burned.
7. He had invented a device that allowed a cavalryman to remove his saber and scabbard from his belt easily.
8. $2,600.
9. John Bell Hood.
10. $110,500.
11. To the citizens of Fredericksburg after the battle.
12. Ambrose P. Hill. He never paid him back.
13. $10,000.
14. To the needy in Fredericksburg.
15. Robert E. Lee.
16. Three banks raised $20,000. The demand for clothing was not met.
17. Richard Ewell.
18. $220,000 in cash.
19. John Bell Hood.
20. Stonewall Jackson. He is on a $500 bill, the most expensive bill.

ꓛRank

1. Who became the youngest officer in the cavalry to attain the rank of major general?
2. What Prussian aristocrat was a member of Jeb Stuart's staff?
3. Which three generals attained the rank of lieutenant general without military training?
4. Who served as the personal staff of Robert E. Lee?
5. What command was Richard Ewell given when he was removed from command of the Second Corps?
6. In what four battles did Richard Ewell have field command?
7. Who were the seven infantry corps commanders during the four-year existence of the Army of Northern Virginia?
8. Who was given command of all the cavalry on July 25, 1862?
9. Who was the commander of the First Corps?
10. After being promoted to lieutenant general what did Richard Ewell do before he reported to Robert E. Lee?
11. Who was the youngest West Point graduate to achieve the rank of major general?
12. Who commanded the Third Corps?
13. Who was confirmed as a brigadier general on May 31, 1864, the day after he had died?
14. Who was the commander of the Petersburg Home Guard?
15. In 1864, who was the commander of the Department of Western Virginia?
16. Who was Jefferson Davis's first secretary of state?
17. What act did Jefferson Davis sign into law on September 18, 1862?
18. How many Virginians rose to the rank of major general?
19. How many Virginians became brigadier generals?
20. What did George Washington Custis Lee do during the war?
21. Under law how many general officers commanded the artillery of the Army of Northern Virginia?
22. Who was the youngest brigadier general?
23. Who was the youngest lieutenant general?
24. Who served as lieutenant generals under Robert E. Lee?
25. Who created the rank of lieutenant general?
26. Whose wife usually required a direct order from Robert E. Lee to leave the lines before a battle?
27. Which general was once assigned to a department made up of the coasts of South Carolina, Georgia, and eastern Florida?
28. Whom did John Pelham give command of the Stuart Horse Artillery?
29. Who was the only division commander in Lee's army who did not graduate from West Point?

Rank (answers)

1. William Henry Fitzhugh Lee.
2. Heros Von Borcke.
3. Wade Hampton and Richard Taylor. Nathan Bedford Forrest was the other.
4. Armistead Long, Charles Marshall, Walter Taylor, and Charles Venable.
5. Department of Richmond.
6. Cross Keys, Second Winchester, Fort Harrison, and Sailor's Creek. The first three were victories.
7. James Longstreet, Stonewall Jackson, Ambrose P. Hill, Jubal Early, Richard Ewell, John Gordon, and Richard Anderson.
8. Jeb Stuart.
9. James Longstreet.
10. Married Lizinka Campbell Brown.
11. Stephen Ramseur.
12. Ambrose P. Hill.
13. James Terrill.
14. Henry Wise.
15. John C. Breckinridge.
16. Robert Toombs. He served until he was appointed a brigadier general in July 1861.
17. An act that made for the appointment of lieutenant generals. It also provided for the creation of the corps.
18. 23.
19. 71.
20. He served as an aide to Jefferson Davis and commanded Richmond's local defense troops.
21. Three.
22. William Paul Roberts. He was 19 in 1861 when he enlisted in the 19th North Carolina Volunteers.
23. Stephen Lee.
24. James Longstreet, Thomas Jackson, Richard Ewell, Ambrose P. Hill, Richard Anderson, and Jubal Early.
25. Congress. Jackson and Longstreet were the first promoted.
26. Ambrose P. Hill's wife.
27. Robert E. Lee.
28. Thomas Rosser.
29. Robert Rodes. He had graduated from the Virginia Military Institute in 1848.

☩Health

1. Which general ate something called frumenty?
2. Which general likely contracted venereal disease while at West Point?
3. What often caused Daniel H. Hill pain?
4. Who was the only lieutenant general not wounded during the war?
5. Which general spoke with a lisp?
6. Which general had such bad asthma that he had to sleep in an upright position?
7. What did John Bell Hood use after his amputation to deal with pain?
8. Who had to wear a slipper during the Battle of Antietam because of a blister on his heel?
9. Which general entered Maryland riding in an ambulance?
10. Who made Richard Ewell's first wooden leg?
11. Who carried a spare wooden leg with him in case of an emergency?
12. Which general was almost deaf?
13. Who suffered from dyspepsia or more likely a stomach ulcer?
14. What was the end result of Richard Ewell's wound received during the Battle of Groveton?
15. What could have been the cause for Lee's brief illness during the second day of the Battle of Gettysburg?
16. Which general suffered from arthritis?
17. Which general had a milk cow attached to his headquarters wagon?
18. During May 1864 which general had an intestinal ailment?
19. What happened to Roger Pryor during the surrender ceremonies at Fort Sumter?
20. Who never took pepper in his food?
21. Who was the only general to survive the war with no major illness or injury?
22. When Robert E. Lee was ill during March 1863 what nickname did his staff give him?
23. Who swore to his mother that he would never drink liquor?
24. In the fall of 1861 whom did Nathan Evans bring up on charges of being drunk?
25. Who produced a flask of whiskey during the Battle of Cross Keys?

❧Health (answers)

1. Richard Ewell. Frumenty was raisins, egg yolks, wheat grain, and sugar boiled in milk.
2. Ambrose P. Hill.
3. A spinal ailment.
4. Richard Anderson.
5. Richard Ewell.
6. William Walker.
7. Laudanum.
8. James Longstreet.
9. Robert E. Lee.
10. Dr. Bundy of New Orleans.
11. John Bell Hood.
12. Theophilus Holmes.
13. Richard Ewell.
14. His leg was amputated.
15. A lad named Leighton Parks brought him fresh raspberries.
16. Jubal Early.
17. William Mahone.
18. Robert E. Lee.
19. He accidentally drank some iodine of potassium. A stomach pump saved his life.
20. Stonewall Jackson. He said it made his left leg ache.
21. Richard Anderson.
22. "The Tycoon."
23. Jeb Stuart. Even as he lay dying he took only one sip.
24. William Barksdale. The only way that he could have the charges dropped was to promise not to drink during the rest of the war.
25. John M. Jones.

⚑Quirks

1. Who never took pepper in his food?
2. Whose brigade did Stonewall Jackson have arrested for burning fence palings?
3. Who walked with a stoop and chewed tobacco all the time?
4. On the march into Maryland who was arguing about who had control over the Federal ambulances captured at Second Bull Run?
5. Why did Stonewall Jackson relieve A.P. Hill of command on the trip into Maryland?
6. Which general shifted tobacco from one side of his jaw to the other when he was excited?
7. Who would not write a letter on a Sunday or even mail a letter that would be in transit on a Sunday?
8. Who took with him at all times his prayer book and table and a bell to call the troops to worship?
9. What three battles did Stonewall Jackson fight on a Sunday?
10. Who had his own private milk cow tied to his headquarters wagon?
11. Whom did Stonewall Jackson have arrested for retreating during the Battle of Kernstown?
12. What made James Longstreet give up gambling?
13. How could you tell when Robert E. Lee was angered?

✎ Quirks (answers)

1. Stonewall Jackson. He said it made his left leg ache.
2. Maxcy Gregg's.
3. Jubal Early.
4. John Bell Hood and Stonewall Jackson.
5. He did not enforce strict marching order of the generals under him.
6. Jubal Early.
7. Stonewall Jackson.
8. Stonewall Jackson.
9. Kernstown, Winchester, and Cross Keys.
10. William Mahone.
11. Richard Garnett.
12. The death of three of his children due to scarlet fever.
13. His face and neck reddened.

Succession

1. When Leonidas Polk was killed who did Joseph Johnston say should replace him?
2. Who took over for James Longstreet after he was wounded in the Wilderness?
3. Who replaced Stonewall Jackson as commander of the Second Corps?
4. When John Bell Hood was transferred to another army who replaced him?
5. Who succeeded Stonewall Jackson as commander of the Stonewall Brigade?
6. When Joseph Johnston was wounded whom did his command fall on?
7. When Charles Winder was mortally wounded who assumed command of the Stonewall Brigade?
8. When Robert E. Lee enlarged his army from two to three corps who was promoted from brigadier general to major general?
9. On January 28, 1865, who was named general in chief of all Confederate armies?
10. On May 26, 1862, this general was promoted to major general. This made him the youngest major general in the army. Who is he?
11. Whom did Wade Hampton succeed as commander of the cavalry corps?
12. Who became the Army of Northern Virginia's third chieftain?
13. Who took command of the Second Corps to replace the ill Richard Ewell?
14. Who took over Jubal Early's division when he was promoted to lieutenant general?
15. Who was the youngest of the eight full generals?
16. Who took over for Henry Heth when he was wounded at Gettysburg?
17. When Gustavus Woodson Smith resigned as commander of the Department of Virginia and North Carolina who took his place?
18. When Edward Porter Alexander was promoted to brigadier general what was he given command of?
19. Who was appointed to fill the command of "Grumble Jones"?
20. Who took command of William Barksdale's Mississippi Brigade after his death at the Battle of Gettysburg?
21. Who took command after Jeb Stuart was mortally wounded at Yellow Tavern?
22. Who were the three commanders of the Second Corps after the death of Stonewall Jackson?

✎Succession (answers)

1. Richard Ewell.
2. Richard Anderson. He would lead the First Corps until October 1864 when Longstreet returned.
3. Richard Ewell.
4. Charles Field.
5. Richard Garnett.
6. Gustavus Smith.
7. William Taliaferro.
8. Henry Heth and Dorsey Pender.
9. Robert E. Lee.
10. Ambrose P. Hill.
11. Jeb Stuart.
12. Robert E. Lee.
13. Jubal Early.
14. Stephen Ramseur.
15. John Bell Hood.
16. James Pettigrew.
17. James Longstreet.
18. Artillery of the First Corps.
19. Bradley Johnson.
20. Brigadier General Benjamin Humphreys.
21. Fitzhugh Lee.
22. Richard Ewell, Jubal Early, and John Gordon.

ᛈ᛫ᚻonors

1. What did Robert E. Lee give to William Roberts on his becoming the youngest general?
2. Which generals have busts in the Hall of Fame?
3. Who were the honorary pallbearers at Stonewall Jackson's funeral?
4. Who was the first president of the South Carolina Agricultural Mechanical Society?
5. Who was the only South Carolinian to lead a corps in the Army of Northern Virginia?
6. Who carried Robert E. Lee's note to John Brown at Harpers Ferry?
7. Which was the only brigade to have an official name?
8. Who was the only officer Robert E. Lee addressed by his given name?
9. Who signed Robert E. Lee's amnesty bill?
10. Why did the citizens of Lynchburg give a filigree sword to John McCausland in 1864?
11. Who drew a map of the Shenandoah Valley for Stonewall Jackson after his defeat at Kernstown?
12. Who was the guard of honor at Jefferson Davis's funeral?
13. Who was once commissioner of the Gettysburg National Military Park?
14. Who administered the oath of office to Jefferson Davis?
15. Who was made an honorary captain and aide-de-camp on the staff of Stonewall Jackson for supplying him with information during the Valley campaign?
16. What did Governor John Letcher give Jeb Stuart for his ride around George McClellan?
17. Whom is Fort Benning named after?
18. Who planted the American flag on the walls of Chapultepec during the Mexican War?
19. Who was United States Minister to Turkey under President Rutherford B. Hayes?
20. Who once held the post of commander in chief of the United Confederate Veterans?
21. In February 1863, who was voted an honorary member of the Virginia House of Delegates?
22. Who was Mississippi's first postwar governor?
23. Who was the only Southern member of the electoral commission that decided the presidential election of 1876?
24. At whose funeral were four of the pallbearers former generals in the Union army, and four were generals in the Confederate army?

✎Honors (answers)

1. His gauntlets.
2. Robert E. Lee and Stonewall Jackson.
3. Richard Ewell, James Longstreet, Arnold Elzey, Richard Garnett, and George Pickett.
4. Johnson Hagood.
5. Richard Anderson.
6. Jeb Stuart.
7. On May 30, 1863, the First Brigade became the Stonewall Brigade.
8. Henry Heth.
9. President Gerald Ford in 1976.
10. For his defense of the city.
11. Jedediah Hotchkiss.
12. James Lane.
13. Lunsford Lomax.
14. Howell Cobb.
15. Belle Boyd.
16. A sword.
17. Henry Benning.
18. George Pickett.
19. James Longstreet.
20. John Gordon.
21. Ambrose P. Hill.
22. Benjamin Humphreys.
23. Eppa Hunton.
24. Cadmus Wilcox's.

25. Who is buried beneath his statue on Monument Avenue in Richmond?
26. Who was the youngest lieutenant general?
27. Cullen Battle was elected to Congress in 1868. Why was he not allowed to serve?
28. Who was president of the American Bar Association in 1882?
29. Who declined the posts of secretary of the treasury and postmaster general under President James Buchanan?
30. Of which two organizations was Jubal Early an officer after the war?
31. Who made Antonia Ford an honorary aide-de-camp on October 7, 1861?
32. Which organization is a nonprofit organization that owns and operates Stratford Hall Plantation?
33. Why did William Wickham resign from the army?
34. Which organization had its first meeting on October 12, 1870, the date of which general's death?

25. Ambrose P. Hill.
26. Stephen Lee.
27. Because he would not take the ironclad oath.
28. Alexander Lawton.
29. Lawrence Branch.
30. Association of the Army of Northern Virginia, and the Southern Historical Society.
31. Jeb Stuart. He gave her this commission because of her espionage activities.
32. Robert E. Lee Memorial Association. Stratford Hall is the birthplace of Robert E. Lee.
33. To serve in the Confederate Congress.
34. Lee Memorial Association. Their goal was to establish a monument to Robert E. Lee in Richmond.

🏳 Books

Match the book with the author in the right-hand column.

1. *The Battle of Seven Pines*
2. *History of the Ninth Virginia Cavalry in the War Between the States*
3. *Memoirs of the War of Secession*
4. *Memoirs of Robert E. Lee*
5. *Reminiscences of the Civil War*
6. *From Manassas to Appomattox*
7. *Military Memoirs of a Confederate*
8. *Autobiographical Sketch and Narrative of the War Between the States*
9. *Rifles and Rifle Practice*
10. *Advance and Retreat*
11. *The War With Mexico*
12. *An Inquiry Into the Law of Negro Slavery in the United States*

a. Armistead Long
b. James Longstreet
c. Jubal Early
d. Thomas R.R. Cobb
e. Gustavus Smith
f. Roswell Ripley
g. Johnson Hagood
h. Cadmus Wilcox
i. Edward Porter Alexander
j. Richard Beale
k. John Gordon
l. John Bell Hood

13. Who once sent Stonewall Jackson a book entitled *Napoleon's Maxims of War*?
14. Who was the editor of the 12-volume *Confederate Military History* published in 1899?
15. Whose autobiographical memoir is the rarest and most sought after book associated with the Army of Northern Virginia?
16. Who edited *The Land We Love*, and *The Southern Home*?
17. Who carried with him at all times his prayer book and a copy of Army Regulations?
18. Who was Stonewall Jackson's chaplain and biographer?
19. Who was the highest ranking officer at Gettysburg to write about the battle?
20. What book did Robert E. Lee read daily?

✎ Books (answers)

1. e
2. j
3. g
4. a
5. k
6. b
7. i
8. c
9. h
10. l
11. f
12. d
13. Jeb Stuart. The book is now in the Museum of the Confederacy in Richmond.
14. Clement Evans.
15. Eppa Hunton.
16. Daniel H. Hill.
17. Jeb Stuart.
18. Robert Lewis Dabney.
19. James Longstreet.
20. The Episcopal *Book of Common Prayer*.

♫Quotes

Who said the following quotes?

1. "God's will be done! I trust He will raise up someone in his place."
2. "These men are going to stay here, General, till the sun goes down or victory is won!"
3. "Up, men, and to your posts! Don't forget today that you are from Old Virginia."
4. "If this valley is lost, Virginia is lost."
5. "He has lost his left arm, but I have lost my right arm."
6. "I shall come out of this fight a live major general or a dead brigadier."
7. Petersburg would be defended to the death "on every street, and around every temple of God and altar of men."
8. "If he gets there it will become a siege, and then it will be a mere question of time."
9. "I fear they may continue to make these changes till they find someone whom I don't understand."
10. "General—he who does not see the hand of God in this is blind, sir, blind."
11. "I know not how to replace him."
12. "That old man had my division massacred."
13. "It's all my fault."
14. "The shot that struck me down is the very best that has been fired for the Southern cause yet."
15. "It is well that war is so terrible we should grow too fond of it."
16. "This monument erected by their father. God only knows which was right."
17. "That is the last council of war I will ever hold."
18. "There is Jackson standing like a stone wall."
19. "Let us cross over the river and rest under the shade of the trees."
20. "Never take counsel of your fears."
21. "He never brought me a false piece of information."
22. "My friends, how do you like this way of coming back into the Union?"
23. "Richmond must not be given up; it shall never be given up."
24. "God has been very kind to us this day."

✎Quotes (answers)

1. Dorsey Pender on the death of Stonewall Jackson.
2. John B. Gordon during the Battle of Antietam.
3. George Pickett said this to his men just before the fateful charge.
4. Stonewall Jackson to a friend.
5. Robert E. Lee on Jackson's amputation.
6. Abner Perrin during the Battle of Spotsylvania. He was shot from his horse while leading a charge.
7. Henry Wise on defending Petersburg.
8. Robert E. Lee to Jubal Early. He was referring to Grant's getting to the James River.
9. Robert E. Lee on learning of McClellan's being replaced by Ambrose Burnside. He said this to James Longstreet.
10. Stonewall Jackson to Richard Ewell after Port Republic.
11. Robert E. Lee on the death of Stonewall Jackson.
12. George Pickett on Robert E. Lee. He was referring to Pickett's Charge.
13. Robert E. Lee shortly after Pickett's Charge.
14. Joseph E. Johnston on his being wounded.
15. Robert E. Lee said this to James Longstreet during the Battle of Fredericksburg.
16. On the monument over the graves of William and James Terrill. William Terrill rose to become a Union brigadier general, who was killed at Perryville in 1862. James Terrill rose to become a Confederate brigadier general, who was killed at Bethesda Church in 1864.
17. Thomas Jackson during the Valley campaign.
18. Barnard E. Bee on Thomas Jackson during the First Battle of Manassas.
19. Stonewall Jackson on his deathbed.
20. Thomas Jackson while at West Point.
21. Robert E. Lee on the death of Jeb Stuart.
22. William Smith on entering York, Pennsylvania.
23. Robert E. Lee on being asked where the army could retreat to if it had to in May 1862.
24. Stonewall Jackson said this as he looked over the cornfield at Antietam.

𝔅Lasts

1. Whose brigade fired the last volley at Appomattox?
2. Who was the last major general to die?
3. Who won the last cavalry victory of the Army of Northern Virginia?
4. What was Ambrose P. Hill's last communication with Stonewall Jackson?
5. What battle was Clement Evans' last as a regimental commander?
6. What was Thomas R.R. Cobb's first and last battle experience as a general officer?
7. Who was the last West Point graduate to die during the war?
8. Who won the last victory in Virginia?
9. Who was the last appointed and youngest of the full generals?
10. Who was the last major general assigned to Lee's command?
11. Who commanded the last troops to leave Richmond?
12. Who was the last officer to receive the rank of brigadier general?
13. Who drew the last line of battle at Appomattox?
14. Whose appointment to brigadier general was made after the Senate adjourned for the last time?
15. On August 12, 1864, whom did Robert E. Lee appoint as commander of the cavalry?
16. Who was the last general to die as a result of battle wounds?
17. Who was the last uniformed man to cross the Mayo Bridge during the evacuation of Richmond?
18. Who led the last charge at Appomattox?
19. Who led the brigade that led the last tactical offensive tried by the Army of Northern Virginia?
20. Which general's division made the last captures at Appomattox?
21. What was the last great offensive made by the Army of Northern Virginia?
22. What battle was Stonewall Jackson's last?
23. What was John Gordon's last major action of the war?
24. Whose brigade was the last to reach the soil of Virginia after the Maryland campaign?
25. Who was Jeb Stuart's last adjutant and first biographer?

✏️Lasts (answers)

1. William Cox on April 9, 1865.
2. Evander Law. He died on October 31, 1920.
3. Thomas Rosser. It occurred at High Bridge.
4. He promised to keep word of Stonewall Jackson's being wounded from the men.
5. Battle of the Wilderness.
6. Battle of Fredericksburg.
7. Ambrose P. Hill.
8. Rufus Barringer. It occurred at Chamberlain Run on March 31, 1865.
9. John Bell Hood.
10. Bryan Grimes on February 15, 1865.
11. Martin Gary.
12. William Perry.
13. Edward Porter Alexander.
14. Theodore Brevard.
15. Wade Hampton.
16. James Dearing was mortally wounded on April 6, 1865. He died on April 23.
17. Walter Stevens.
18. John Gordon.
19. Philip Cook.
20. Clement Evans'.
21. Battle of Gettysburg.
22. Chancellorsville.
23. On March 25, 1865, he directed the predawn attack on Fort Stedman.
24. Jubal Early's.
25. Major Henry B. McClellan.

☐Trivial

1. Who acted as an arbitrator over a boundary dispute between Costa Rica and Nicaragua during 1897 to 1900?
2. Who once had as a tutor Salmon P. Chase, the future secretary of the treasury and chief justice of the United States Supreme Court?
3. When Mrs. John Gordon was seen going to the rear, what did this mean?
4. Whose men marched 646 miles in 48 days?
5. Which state contributed the most men who became generals?
6. What did Harry Hays suggest be used to drum disgruntled soldiers out of the army?
7. Who kept a banjo player on his headquarters staff?
8. Who was the most photographed of the lieutenant generals?
9. Who raised the unit called Cobb's Legion?
10. Who was born on April 12, 1831, thirty years prior to the firing on Fort Sumter?
11. Who arrived too late for the Battle of First Bull Run due to a railroad accident?
12. Who organized the Lynchburg Home Guards in 1859?
13. Who entered the army as an aide to Richard Ewell?
14. Who rode into a swarm of wasps during the First Battle of First Bull Run?
15. Who was the groom in Henry Heth's wedding in April 1857?
16. Who led the Virginia Military Institute cadets at the hanging of John Brown?
17. Who served as a presidential elector for John Bell in 1860?
18. Who spent most of the war as an aide to Jefferson Davis?
19. Whom did Robert E. Lee serve as an adviser early in the war?
20. Who was Stonewall Jackson's engineer during the Romney campaign?
21. What company of volunteers did John Gordon raise?
22. Who developed the wigwag system of signaling in the military?
23. What once saved the life of Goode Bryan during battle?
24. What once stopped a musket ball from killing Sandie Pendleton?
25. Where was the headquarters of Thomas J. Jackson during the Valley campaign?
26. Who usually wrote Robert E. Lee's orders?
27. As the Confederate army marched away from Richmond in May 1862, which general planted artillery shells in the roads as land mines against the Federals?
28. When did Robert E. Lee grow his beard?

❧Trivial (answers)

1. Edward Porter Alexander. He was appointed by President Grover Cleveland.
2. Lawrence O'Bryan Branch.
3. That action was about to begin.
4. Stonewall Jackson's men during the Valley campaign.
5. North Carolina.
6. The tune "Yankee Doodle."
7. Jeb Stuart.
8. John Bell Hood.
9. Thomas R.R. Cobb.
10. George Anderson.
11. George T. Anderson.
12. Samuel Garland, Jr.
13. Fitzhugh Lee.
14. William Barksdale.
15. Ambrose P. Hill.
16. Thomas Jackson.
17. Rufus Barringer.
18. George Washington Custis Lee.
19. Jefferson Davis.
20. Seth Barton.
21. The Raccoon Roughs.
22. Edward Porter Alexander.
23. A silver spectacle case once deflected a bullet.
24. A knife in his pants pocket.
25. Winchester, Virginia.
26. Colonel Charles Marshall.
27. Gabriel Rains.
28. While he was in western Virginia in the early fall of 1861.

29. Which general was part Cherokee?
30. Which general was married five times?
31. Why did James Walker once challenge Thomas Jackson to a duel?
32. Which brigadier general resigned his commission to occupy his seat in the Confederate House of Representatives?
33. Which general outfought Generals James Shields, Nathaniel Banks, Robert H. Milroy, and John C. Fremont in the Shenandoah Valley?
34. Which general had a campaign in the Shenandoah Valley that prevented the reinforcement of George McClellan outside of Richmond?
35. Who gave Stonewall Jackson command of the First Brigade of Virginia troops?
36. Which general was one of the main designers of the Confederate Constitution?
37. Which future general voted against the ordinance of secession?
38. On June 4, 1861, who proposed to Robert E. Lee to attack Federal forces at Hagerstown, Maryland?
39. How many times during the war did Robert E. Lee make a speech?
40. Under whom was John Mosby once a cavalry scout?

29. Henry Benning.
30. John Imboden.
31. Because Jackson had him dismissed from the Virginia Military Institute.
32. Williams Wickham.
33. Stonewall Jackson.
34. Stonewall Jackson.
35. Joseph E. Johnston.
36. Thomas R.R. Cobb.
37. Jubal Early.
38. Isaac Trimble.
39. Only once. This was when he accepted command of Virginia's military and naval forces.
40. Jeb Stuart.

♜Wounds

1. Who received eleven wounds during the war, five of them occurring during the Battle of Chancellorsville?
2. Whose amputated leg was buried in the garden of Arris Buckner's house?
3. Which general was hit in the leg by a rifle ball that had killed his horse?
4. When Jeb Stuart was wounded at Yellow Tavern what was he armed with?
5. How many times had John R. Cooke been wounded by the time he was promoted to brigadier general?
6. Why did Robert E. Lee cancel the promotion of John Barry to brigadier general on August 13, 1864?
7. When he was wounded during the Battle of Fair Oaks which general had the bullet removed from his foot while he sat on his horse?
8. Which general refused to leave the battlefield without his grandfather's Revolutionary War sword after he was wounded?
9. When Roswell Ripley was struck in the neck by a minie ball, what deflected it?
10. During the Battle of Groveton, whose knee was shattered by a minie ball?
11. Who gave his field glasses to Lieutenant Theodore C. Garnett after he was wounded?
12. After which battle was John Bell Hood's leg amputated?
13. Which general lost his right foot at the Battle of Brandy Station?
14. Which general lost the use of his left arm during the Battle of Gettysburg?
15. Who amputated Stonewall Jackson's left arm?
16. While recuperating after the loss of his leg which general was often seen in the poker dens in Richmond?
17. Who bled to death from a wound in the thigh after the Battle of Fredericksburg?
18. Whose leg did Dr. Hunter Holmes McGuire amputate after the Battle of Groveton?
19. Who lost a foot as the result of a wound received during the Battle of Spotsylvania?
20. Which general was wounded by a minie ball during the Battle of Monocacy that drove his sewing kit into his side?
21. Which general had his hands injured from a fall while trying to steady his horse?
22. When James Longstreet was wounded at Chapultepec to whom did he hand the colors?

✎Wounds (answers)

1. William Cox.
2. Richard Ewell.
3. Arnold Elzey.
4. A Northern-made 0.36 caliber Whitney Revolver.
5. Seven.
6. Due to a wound that disabled him.
7. Wade Hampton.
8. Joseph E. Johnston.
9. His cravat.
10. Richard Ewell's.
11. Jeb Stuart.
12. Battle of Chickamauga.
13. Matthew Butler.
14. John Bell Hood.
15. Dr. Hunter Holmes McGuire.
16. John Bell Hood.
17. Thomas R.R. Cobb.
18. Richard Ewell.
19. Henry Walker.
20. Clement A. Evans. Pins would be picked out of the wound for years.
21. Robert E. Lee. The fall occurred as he was trying to calm Traveller, who had shied.
22. George Pickett.

23. Who was "wounded" in his wooden leg during the Battle of Gettysburg?
24. Whose thigh was fractured by a bullet during the Battle of Chickamauga?
25. Was Jeb Stuart ever touched by a bullet before he was mortally wounded?
26. Which general's wound, caused by artillery fire during the Battle of Brandy Station, resulted in the amputation of his right leg?
27. Who once had half his mustache shot off by a minie ball?
28. Who had a maimed left hand that was the result of a shooting accident?

23. Richard Ewell.
24. John Bell Hood.
25. No. But his uniform coat had been cut once.
26. Matthew Butler.
27. Jeb Stuart.
28. Lafayette McLaws.

☘Death

1. Which general died on October 16, 1862, from a wound received during the Battle of Antietam?
2. Who was the last surviving major general?
3. Who died on July 5, 1863, on the George Spangler Farm in Gettysburg, Pennsylvania?
4. Who was killed while checking his lines at Bethesda Church on June 2, 1864?
5. Who committed suicide on December 2, 1861?
6. Which general died on April 9, 1892, the 27th anniversary of the surrender of Appomattox?
7. What was Gabriel Wharton wearing when he was buried?
8. Who was the last general to die as a direct result of battle wounds?
9. Who died from pneumonia, not from the amputation of his left arm?
10. Who was temporarily buried in the yard of the house in which Stonewall Jackson would die?
11. Before he died to whom did Maxcy Gregg give his dress sword?
12. Who was the last of the high command to die?
13. Which general had his obituary appear prematurely in the *New York Herald* in February 1865?
14. Which general had a daughter who was born on October 17, 1862, the day after he died?
15. A map of the defenses of Richmond was found on the body of which dead general?
16. Richard Ewell died on January 25, 1872. Who had died three days before him?
17. Which general's three children died from scarlet fever?
18. Who was killed at Fredericksburg while trying to rally his men?
19. Who died at Belle Grove, the headquarters of the Union General Phil Sheridan?
20. At whose deathbed did George Custer and Wesley Merritt sit?
21. Which general, killed at Antietam, would be buried next to his son?
22. The hymn "Rock of Ages" was sung to which general as he lay dying?
23. Which general died in the lobby of the Fifth Avenue Hotel in New York City?
24. Which general died on October 20, 1864, the day after he learned that his daughter had been born?
25. What did Private John Deal do for John Bell Hood?
26. On what day of the week did Stonewall Jackson die?
27. During which battle were Brigadier Generals Abner Perrin and Junius Daniel killed?

✎Death (answers)

1. George B. Anderson was shot near the joint in the ankle. Shortly after the amputation infection set in.
2. Evander Law died in 1920.
3. Lewis Armistead.
4. George Doles.
5. Philip St. George Cocke.
6. Charles Field.
7. The colors of the 51st Virginia.
8. James Dearing. He died on April 23 from a wound received on April 6, 1865.
9. Stonewall Jackson.
10. Elisha Paxton, who had been killed on May 3, 1863.
11. Captain Alexander Haskell, his staff officer.
12. James Longstreet died on January 2, 1904.
13. Gilbert Sorrel.
14. George B. Anderson.
15. John R. Chambliss.
16. His wife.
17. James Longstreet.
18. Maxcy Gregg.
19. Stephen Ramseur.
20. Stephen Ramseur.
21. William Starke. His son had been killed during the Battle of Seven Pines.
22. Jeb Stuart.
23. Howell Cobb.
24. Stephen Ramseur.
25. He saved his life on May 7, 1862. He shot a Federal soldier who was aiming at the general.
26. On a Sunday, as he had wished.
27. Spotsylvania.

28. Whom did Jeb Stuart tell that he did not expect to outlive the war, and that he did not want to survive if the South lost the war?
29. Who died on his way to court in 1875?
30. Which two generals called on Ambrose P. Hill while on their deathbed?
31. Who once said that he preferred to be killed while leading a cavalry charge?
32. Whom did Alexander Pendleton dress for burial?
33. Who was killed by a hired killer on August 14, 1880?
34. Who called for Ambrose P. Hill while on their deathbed?

28. Major Andrew Venable.
29. Henry Benning.
30. Stonewall Jackson and Robert E. Lee.
31. Jeb Stuart.
32. Stonewall Jackson.
33. Bryan Grimes. He had tried to expel undesirables from the local community. They retaliated.
34. Both Robert E. Lee and Stonewall Jackson.

♭Seven Days

1. Why did George B. Anderson command Winfield Featherston's brigade during the Battle of Seven Pines?
2. Who owned the White House, the former home of Martha Custis Washington?
3. Who went up in a balloon during the Battle of Gaines' Mills?
4. Who was the only brigadier general killed during the Battle of Malvern Hill?
5. Who lost the use of his right arm after Seven Pines?
6. At which battle was James Conner's leg broken by a rifle ball?
7. Who was Robert E. Lee's opponent during the Seven Days battles?
8. Who started the Battle of Mechanicsville?
9. When was Robert E. Lee's first victory?
10. How many men did Jeb Stuart take with him in his ride around the Union army?
11. The Battle of Gaines' Mill started at 2:00 p.m., on June 27, 1862 when A.P. Hill attacked forces under which general?
12. Who had his pistol handle shot off during the Battle of Malvern Hill?
13. Where was Jeb Stuart sent on June 12, 1862?
14. Why was Stonewall Jackson six hours late for battle on June 26?
15. Whom did Ambrose P. Hill send to the rear after the Battle of White Oak Swamp?
16. Who immediately replaced Joseph E. Johnston when he was wounded during the Battle of Seven Pines?
17. Who was unhorsed during the Battle of Gaines' Mill, with a bullet in the shoulder?
18. Who wrote, "It was not war—it was murder"?
19. How did Lee reorganize the army after the Seven Days?
20. Who had never led men in combat before the Seven Days?
21. Who was John Bankhead Magruder's chief of artillery?
22. On the retreat from Williamsburg what did Gabriel Rains do to the roads?
23. Who was wounded, captured, and sent to a Federal prison during the Battle of Fair Oaks?
24. Who had a bullet removed from his foot while on the battlefield at Fair Oaks?
25. Who were the only two general officers not wounded at Fair Oaks?
26. Who left the Shenandoah Valley with a pass made out for an unidentified colonel, when he went to meet with Robert E. Lee?
27. What did Ambrose P. Hill call his command?
28. Who was left behind to watch George McClellan's withdrawal from the Peninsula after the Seven Days?

Seven Days (answers)

1. Winfield Featherston was sick.
2. William Henry Fitzhugh "Rooney" Lee.
3. Edward Porter Alexander.
4. Richard Griffith.
5. James J. Pettigrew.
6. Gaines' Mill.
7. George McClellan.
8. Ambrose P. Hill.
9. Seven Pines or Fair Oaks.
10. 1,200 men.
11. Fitz John-Porter.
12. John B. Gordon. It also pierced his canteen, and tore away part of the front of his coat.
13. He was sent on a reconnaissance to find out how far north of the Chickahominy River Fitz John-Porter's corps extended. This resulted in the ride around McClellan.
14. Because of high water and rains.
15. Jefferson Davis and Robert E. Lee.
16. Gustavus W. Smith. He was assigned by President Jefferson Davis.
17. George Pickett.
18. Daniel H. Hill on the Battle of Malvern Hill.
19. He decreased Stonewall Jackson's brigades from fourteen to seven, and increased James Longstreet's from six to twenty-eight.
20. Robert E. Lee.
21. George W. Randolph, grandson of Thomas Jefferson.
22. Planted land mines in the road.
23. Johnston Pettigrew.
24. Wade Hampton.
25. Evander Law and John Bell Hood.
26. Stonewall Jackson.
27. The Light Division.
28. Richard Anderson.

29. Who, at the Battle of Mechanicsville, attacked without waiting for Jackson to arrive, or without orders from Lee?
30. From March 23 to June 9, 1862, who defeated three Federal armies in five battles in the Shenandoah Valley?
31. During which battle was Jubal Early wounded on May 5, 1862?
32. What did James Longstreet send to Richmond as a trophy after the Battle of Frayser's Farm?
33. During the Battle of Malvern Hill who was knocked from his chair at a camp table by an exploding shell?
34. What was Robert E. Lee's first major order after assuming command of the Army of Northern Virginia?
35. Where was John Bankhead Magruder sent after the Seven Days?
36. What happened to Benjamin Huger after the Seven Days?
37. Who wanted to make a twilight charge up the slope of Malvern Hill?
38. Which general was captured during the Battle of Gaines' Mill and sent to a Federal prison?
39. During the Battle of Kernstown who ordered a retreat when his troops ran out of ammunition?

29. Ambrose P. Hill.
30. Stonewall Jackson.
31. Battle of Williamsburg.
32. Brigadier General George McCall.
33. Daniel H. Hill. Only his coat was injured. It was torn by a bit of metal.
34. To retreat from Seven Pines to the outskirts of Richmond.
35. To command the Department of Texas, New Mexico, and Arizona.
36. He was transferred to the War Department as chief inspector of artillery and ordnance.
37. Isaac Trimble.
38. William Barksdale. He would later be exchanged for Union General John Reynolds.
39. Richard Garnett.

Second Manassas

1. Why did Richard Garnett's court-martial board never reach a verdict?
2. Whom did Robert E. Lee oppose at Second Manassas?
3. What was Lee's aim in the Battle of Second Manassas?
4. Who brought on the Second Battle of Manassas?
5. Whose body did Lee send back to Union lines under a flag of truce?
6. When Lee divided his army after the Seven Days battles, whom did he send to contain Union Major General John Pope in the Shenandoah Valley?
7. Why did Nathan G. Evans order the arrest of John Bell Hood?
8. Which Federal general was intensely disliked by Robert E. Lee?
9. Whose troops arrived for battle on the second day at Manassas, August 30, 1862?
10. During the Battle of First Manassas who wandered into a wasp nest?
11. Before the Second Manassas campaign what did Lee send home to Richmond for safekeeping?
12. What was Lee's first full campaign as commander of the Army of Northern Virginia?
13. During the raid on Verdiersville Jeb Stuart lost his plumed hat. How had the hat originally been acquired?
14. After he lost his famous plumed hat what did Jeb Stuart wear?
15. One of George Taylor's men aimed his gun at which general, firing a minie ball by his head?
16. Who was charged with defending the stone bridge during First Manassas?
17. What did Stonewall Jackson ask for after the First Battle of Manassas?
18. Who resigned during the First Battle of Manassas?
19. On July 27, 1862, why did Robert E. Lee order Ambrose P. Hill to join Stonewall Jackson at Gordonsville?
20. Who succeeded Richard Ewell after he was wounded at Groveton?
21. Who wrote a note to John Pope that read, "General, You have my hat and plume. I have your best coat. I have the honor to propose a cartel for the fair exchange of the prisoners"?

❧Second Manassas (answers)

1. Because the army went into motion in August 1862.
2. John Pope.
3. To evict John Pope from Virginia. It was not to destroy his army.
4. Stonewall Jackson.
5. Union General Phil Kearny.
6. Stonewall Jackson.
7. Because some of John Bell Hood's men had captured some Federal ambulances. Since Hood was on a part of the field where Nathan Evans was in command, Evans ordered him to give the ambulances to his South Carolina troops. Hood refused.
8. General John Pope. This was because of his waging war on civilians.
9. James Longstreet's.
10. William Barksdale.
11. A straw hat and underjacket.
12. Second Manassas.
13. Jeb Stuart had won a bet with Union General Samuel Crawford. Stuart had bet him that the Northern press would declare Cedar Mountain a Union victory.
14. A handkerchief wrapped around his head.
15. Stonewall Jackson.
16. Nathan Evans.
17. 10,000 men with whom to take Washington.
18. Robert Toombs. He resigned as head of the State Department. He went to Georgia to become brigadier general.
19. For a joint strike against John Pope.
20. Alexander Lawton.
21. Jeb Stuart.

♌Antietam

1. Whom did Robert E., Lee oppose at Antietam?
2. At what battle was Samuel Garland killed?
3. How many times was John Gordon wounded?
4. Who died on October 16, 1862, from a wound received in the ankle?
5. What saved the life of Maxcy Gregg?
6. Who led the two corps on the campaign into Maryland?
7. What kept John Gordon from drowning in his own blood?
8. What did Robert E. Lee use as his invasion route into Maryland?
9. On Sunday, September 7, the Reverend Daniel Zacharias offered a prayer to President Abraham Lincoln. Who was in the congregation?
10. What was Jackson's first food of the day on September 17, 1862?
11. Who led the last Confederate defense of the Sunken Road?
12. What was Lee's first objective in the North?
13. Who is suspected of losing his copy of Special Order No. 191?
14. Who wrote Lee's Special Order No. 191 on September 9, 1862?
15. Which brigadier general was wounded in the ankle?
16. Who remembered the battle as "artillery hell"?
17. What did Union Corporal Barton Mitchell do?
18. Which brigadier general was struck by three bullets and died within one hour?
19. Who fired the first shot of the Battle of Antietam?
20. Whose batteries were in front of the Dunker Church?
21. Who allowed his men to cook something on the eve of the battle?
22. Who climbed a tree during the battle to count the enemy flags for Stonewall Jackson?
23. Who protected Lee's rear after the battle?
24. What request did John Bell Hood make to Lee for his men on the eve of the battle?
25. While Ambrose P. Hill was meeting with his three brigadiers, who was killed by a Federal sharpshooter?
26. Whose campaign in the Shenandoah Valley caused the cancellation of the movement of 40,000 Union troops to the peninsula?
27. On the march into Maryland who held a grand ball at Urbana?
28. Why was John Bell Hood marching in the rear during the march into Maryland?
29. While marching into Maryland what was Jackson's order in regards to any man caught leaving the column without an excuse?
30. From whom did Ambrose P. Hill say he received his copy of Special Order No. 191?

✎Antietam (answers)

1. George McClellan.
2. Battle of South Mountain on September 14, 1862.
3. Five.
4. George B. Anderson.
5. A large handkerchief in his pocket.
6. James Longstreet and Stonewall Jackson.
7. A bullet hole in his hat.
8. The Shenandoah Valley.
9. Stonewall Jackson. He had fallen asleep and did not hear the prayer.
10. Peaches. They were given to him by Dr. Hunter McGuire.
11. Daniel H. Hill.
12. To destroy the Pennsylvania Railroad's longbridge over the Susquehanna River at Harrisburg.
13. Daniel H. Hill. He was suspected of receiving two copies.
14. Robert H. Chilton.
15. George B. Anderson. A wound that would prove fatal.
16. Stephen Lee, a colonel at the time of the battle.
17. Found the lost copy of Lee's Special Order No. 191.
18. William Starke.
19. Lieutenant A.W. Garber, a member of one of Stuart's batteries.
20. Stephen Lee's.
21. John Bell Hood. It was the first time in days the men had hot food.
22. Private William Hood.
23. Fitzhugh Lee.
24. That his men be allowed to go to the rear and cook some food. They had had no rations since September 13.
25. Lawrence Branch.
26. Stonewall Jackson's.
27. Jeb Stuart.
28. He was arguing with Jackson over who was entitled to the Federal ambulances that had been captured at Second Manassas.
29. That if caught they would be shot.
30. He said that he had never received the copy sent to him by Adjutant Robert Chilton. Instead he received a copy made for him by Jackson.

31. Whom did Brigadier General Julius White surrender to after the Battle of Maryland Heights?
32. With the death of Brigadier General Lawrence O' Bryan Branch, 10 Confederate generals had been either killed or wounded. Who are they?
33. On the march into Maryland which general had his buttons cut off his coat by admirers in Martinsburg, Virginia?
34. Who was credited with the largest surrender of United States troops during the war?
35. Which two major generals were promoted to lieutenant general after the campaign into Maryland?
36. Who was the only brigadier general to be cited by Lee for promotion to major general after the Battle of Antietam?
37. Who informed Lee that Special Order No. 191 had been found by Union troops?
38. Did James Archer ride in an ambulance at the start of the Maryland campaign?
39. What did James Longstreet claim he did with his copy of Special Order No. 191?
40. How was William Henry Fitzhugh "Rooney" Lee almost captured during the Maryland campaign?

31. Stonewall Jackson.
32. Brigadier General Lawrence Branch, Brigadier General George B. Anderson, Brigadier General William Starke, Major General Richard Anderson, Brigadier General Lewis Armistead, Brigadier General Ambrose R. Wright, Brigadier General Alexander Lawton, Brigadier General John R. Jones, Brigadier General Roswell Ripley and future Brigadier General John Brown Gordon. Gordon was a colonel at the time of the battle. He was promoted for his action at Antietam.
33. Stonewall Jackson.
34. Stonewall Jackson. The surrender occurred at Harpers Ferry on September 15, 1862. He took as prisoners 12,500 soldiers.
35. Stonewall Jackson and James Longstreet.
36. Isaac Trimble.
37. Jeb Stuart.
38. Yes. He was too sick to ride a horse.
39. He said that he tore up and chewed the pieces of Special Order No. 191.
40. While outside of Boonsboro, Maryland his horse fell while crossing a bridge. He was knocked senseless. Crawling to nearby woods saved him from Union cavalry troops.

☞Fredericksburg

1. Who sent a note to Lee that read, "...if he wants a bridge of dead Yankees I can furnish him with one"?
2. During the winter who cut out paper dolls with five-year-old Janie Corbin?
3. Whose brigade held the sunken road in front of Marye's Heights?
4. Who opposed Lee at Fredericksburg?
5. Who was shot through the spine and killed?
6. Who was the division commander on Marye's Heights?
7. Who wrote of Marye's Heights, "A chicken could not live on that field when we open on it"?
8. When did Lee reorganize the army into corps?
9. On December 11, 1862, two Confederate cannon signalled that the Yankees were crossing the Rappahannock River. Whose troops sounded the alarm?
10. Who had his femoral artery cut by a fragment of a shell?
11. Which general once sent a telegram to Chief Quartermaster Montgomery Meigs in Washington, D.C.?
12. Who was accused of hiding behind a tree during the Battle of Fredericksburg?
13. Who commanded the guns on Marye's Heights?
14. After surveying the devastation of Fredericksburg, one of Jackson's staff officers was asked what could be done about this. How did he reply?
15. What did Lee choose as his headquarters when he arrived in Fredericksburg on November 21, 1862?
16. Where did Lee spend most of the Battle of Fredericksburg?
17. During the Fredericksburg campaign who walked along the Rappahannock River at night listening to the Yankee bands?

✎Fredericksburg (answers)

1. William Barksdale.
2. Stonewall Jackson.
3. Joseph Kershaw.
4. Ambrose Burnside.
5. Maxcy Gregg.
6. Lafayette McLaws.
7. Edward Porter Alexander.
8. After Antietam. Both Jackson and Longstreet were promoted to lieutenant general.
9. William Barksdale's Mississippians.
10. Thomas R.R. Cobb.
11. The telegram was from Jeb Stuart. It complained about the quality of the mules that he had captured.
12. John R. Jones.
13. Edward Porter Alexander.
14. "Kill 'em. Kill 'em all."
15. Hamilton's Crossing.
16. Telegraph Hill. This later became known as Lee's Hill.
17. Lafayette McLaws and William Barksdale.

⚐Chancellorsville

1. Whose brigade mortally wounded Stonewall Jackson?
2. To whom did Lee send a supply of condensed milk and whiskey after the battle?
3. After Jackson's death Lee created a Third Corps. Who commanded it?
4. Who had his sword severed by a minie ball?
5. Who immediately took over after Jackson was wounded?
6. Who was given command of the Second Corps on the reorganization?
7. Whom did Lee oppose at Chancellorsville?
8. In January 1863 what did Jackson have Jedediah Hotchkiss do?
9. How many bullets hit Jackson?
10. Who was leading the Stonewall Brigade at the time?
11. Who was given command of the First Corps on the reorganization after the death of Jackson?
12. Who commanded Longstreet's three divisions?
13. Who led Richard Ewell's three divisions?
14. How was Ambrose P. Hill's new corps created?
15. Who commanded Ambrose P. Hill's division after he was wounded at Chancellorsville?
16. During this battle Robert E. Lee ordered what to be done for the first time?
17. While Robert E. Lee and Stonewall Jackson plotted strategy early in the morning on May 2 on what were they seated?
18. Who was Jackson's chief of artillery during this battle?
19. What town did Robert E. Lee tell Richard Ewell to capture if it came within his means?
20. Who held the Union troops at Fredericksburg during the Battle of Chancellorsville?
21. What prompted Jackson to go on his fateful ride?
22. As the generals left their meal at the Chancellor House, what did Jeb Stuart give to Fannie Chancellor?
23. Which two generals held the Federals in check while Jackson made his flank march to attack the Union line on the right?
24. Why did Major General Arnold Elzey, commander of the Department of Richmond, withhold reinforcements from Lieutenant General James Longstreet in April 1863?

🖎 Chancellorsville (answers)

1. John Barry's.
2. To those lying on the field.
3. Ambrose P. Hill.
4. Bryan Grimes.
5. Edward Johnson.
6. Richard Ewell.
7. Joseph Hooker.
8. Draw a detailed map from Winchester to Harrisburg, Pennsylvania.
9. Three. One hit his right palm; one entered his left wrist; and the third splintered the bone of his left arm between the shoulder and elbow.
10. Elisha Franklin Paxton. He was killed at Chancellorsville.
11. James Longstreet.
12. Lafayette McLaws, George Pickett, and John Bell Hood.
13. Jubal Early, Robert Rodes, and Edward Johnson.
14. His corps was created by taking one division away from Jackson, and one division away from Longstreet. A third division was made and given to Henry Heth.
15. William Pender.
16. Erection of field fortifications.
17. Yankee hardtack boxes.
18. Stapleton Crutchfield.
19. Harrisburg, Pennsylvania.
20. Jubal Early.
21. His personal map of the Chancellorsville battlefield was inaccurate.
22. He gave her a gold dollar to remember him by.
23. Richard Anderson and Lafayette McLaws.
24. Because of the bread riots in Richmond.

25. Did Jeb Stuart ever issue a general order congratulating his corps on their victory at Chancellorsville?
26. After Jackson and Ambrose P. Hill were wounded, who was the next senior division commander?
27. Who led a division in combat for the first time during this battle?
28. During the Battle of Chancellorsville who excused himself from the field because of an ulcerated leg?

25. No. Though he did keep the written order in his pocket as long as he lived.
26. Robert Rodes.
27. Robert Rodes.
28. John R. Jones.

🏳️ Gettysburg

1. Whom did Henry Heth send to procure supplies on June 30, 1863?
2. Who made the first contact with Union forces at Gettysburg?
3. Who was sick on the first day?
4. Who ordered the burning of the ironworks owned by Thaddeus Stevens in Greenwood, Pennsylvania?
5. Who fought with his arm in a sling at Gettysburg, the Wilderness, and Spotsylvania?
6. Why was Lee not prepared to bring on a general engagement on July 1, 1863?
7. Whose brigade achieved the northern-most penetration made by the Confederacy during the war?
8. Whom did Lee oppose at Gettysburg?
9. What did a little girl in York, Pennsylvania give to John Gordon?
10. Which regiment, led by Colonel Birkett Fry, had the first contact with Union troops on July 1.
11. What did Lee do with his penknife while he had his headquarters at Cashtown?
12. Where did Richard Ewell raise the Stars and Bars?
13. Which general was left behind to watch Joseph Hooker's army?
14. Which general once demanded the surrender of Carlisle, Pennsylvania?
15. Who was surprised by Brigadier General Alfred Pleasanton at Brandy Station on June 9, 1863?
16. Which general wanted to put the Army of Northern Virginia between Meade and Washington?
17. Whose sword was broken by the same volley that killed him on July 2, 1863?
18. Whose brigade secured Devil's Den on July 2?
19. What did Richard Ewell fail to capture during the first day?
20. What saved Henry Heth from being wounded?
21. Who had his headquarters on June 28 in a grove called Shetter's Woods, outside of Chambersburg?
22. From where did Lee observe the fighting on July 1?
23. Who had a bridle rein cut by a bullet on July 2?
24. Which two generals were whittling sticks when Lee met with his generals on July 2?
25. To whom did John Bell Hood's command pass when he was wounded?
26. Who was shot in his wooden leg during the battle?
27. Who achieved fame because of a failed charge?
28. At what did Edward Porter Alexander fire his 75 guns?

✎ Gettysburg (answers)

1. James Pettigrew.
2. Henry Heth's division.
3. Ambrose P. Hill.
4. Jubal Early.
5. Stephen Ramseur. He had been wounded at Malvern Hill.
6. Longstreet was not there yet.
7. Albert Jenkins. They made it up to a hill four miles from the Pennsylvania capital.
8. George Gordon Meade.
9. A bouquet of roses. Inside was a note that described the Federal forces at Wrightsville.
10. 13th Alabama.
11. He cut out a map of Adams County that was hanging on the wall of the house where he was staying.
12. Carlisle Barracks.
13. Ambrose P. Hill and his Third Corps.
14. Jeb Stuart. He also asked that all women and children leave.
15. Jeb Stuart.
16. James Longstreet. He wanted a defensive battle on ground chosen by Lee and him.
17. William Barksdale.
18. Henry Benning.
19. Cemetery Hill.
20. A few folds of paper inside his hat band.
21. Robert E. Lee.
22. Herr Ridge.
23. Cadmus Wilcox.
24. James Longstreet and Ambrose P. Hill. This was observed by Lieutenant Colonel Arthur Fremantle.
25. Evander Law.
26. Richard Ewell.
27. George Pickett.
28. The Federals on Cemetery Ridge prior to Pickett's Charge.

29. Who was the only general to break through enemy lines during Pickett's Charge?
30. What did Henry Bingham give to General Winfield Scott Hancock?
31. Who was struck in the leg by a piece of cannon shell and died two weeks later?
32. Who was the sole surviving brigadier general of Pickett's Charge?
33. Who rode a horse during Pickett's Charge?
34. Who sent a note to the wife of wounded Union General Francis Barlow?
35. What did Lewis Armistead do with his hat during Pickett's Charge?
36. Who took over command when James Archer was captured?
37. After Pickett's Charge, James Longstreet asked British Colonel Arthur Fremantle for a drink. What did he give him?
38. Whose brigade supported Richard Garnett's and James Kemper's brigades during Pickett's Charge?
39. Who escorted the wagon trains, including the ambulances, in the retreat?
40. Who were the six generals either mortally wounded or killed?
41. Which two generals led corps for the first time during the Battle of Gettysburg?
42. When George Pickett asked if he was to advance his troops on July 3, 1863, how did James Longstreet reply?

29. Lewis Armistead.
30. The spurs, pocketbook, watch, chain, and seal of Lewis Armistead.
31. Dorsey Pender.
32. James Kemper. And he was wounded.
33. James Kemper and Richard Garnett.
34. John Gordon.
35. He held it up in the air on the tip of his sword.
36. Birkett Fry.
37. Rum.
38. Lewis Armistead.
39. John Imboden.
40. Lewis Armistead, William Barksdale, Richard Garnett, Dorsey Pender, James Pettigrew, and Paul Semmes.
41. Richard Ewell and A.P. Hill.
42. All he could do was nod.

⚐On To Richmond

1. In August 1863 who wrote to Jefferson Davis offering to resign?
2. What did Robert E. Lee petition Richmond for?
3. When James Longstreet left the Army of Northern Virginia in September 1863, where did he go?
4. When was the first encounter between Robert E. Lee and Ulysses S. Grant?
5. Whom did Lee choose in 1864 to lead an army down the Shenandoah Valley?
6. Whom did Lee order to capture New Berne in January 1864?
7. Who were the four generals killed at Spotsylvania?
8. Whose troops beat the Federals to Spotsylvania Court House?
9. Where did General Ulysses S. Grant pitch his tent after Spotsylvania?
10. During the Battle of the Wilderness, who, after being fired on by his own troops, almost bled to death?
11. Who was mortally wounded while cheering his men forward at the "Bloody Angle" during the Battle of Spotsylvania?
12. Who had 22 men executed in Kinston, North Carolina?
13. From what did Robert E. Lee direct battle in late May 1864?
14. Who, in January 1864, submitted to the Senate the names of 14 to be confirmed as major general and 56 to be confirmed as brigadier general?
15. Whose men did the firing that wounded James Longstreet?
16. During which battle was James Longstreet wounded?
17. Which general was killed in the same volley that wounded Longstreet?
18. Who was sick during the Battle of the Wilderness?
19. Who was censured by George Pickett for his lack of cooperation at New Berne?
20. In May 1864 Richard Ewell was given indefinite leave because of his health. Who took his place?
21. Who commanded the First Corps after Longstreet was wounded during the Battle of the Wilderness?
22. Whom did General John C. Pemberton defeat on May 15, 1864?
23. Who defeated William Jones at Piedmont on June 5, 1864?
24. Who got closer to Washington, D.C. in 1864 than any other general during four years of war?
25. Who was assigned to the command of the Virginia reserves after he was exchanged as a prisoner of war?
26. Who led the Second Corps into Maryland on July 6, 1864?
27. During the campaign against Washington in 1864, where did Jubal Early have his field headquarters?

✎On To Richmond (answers)

1. Robert E. Lee.
2. Food, shoes, and clothing.
3. He went west to join the army of Braxton Bragg.
4. Battle of the Wilderness.
5. Jubal Early.
6. George Pickett.
7. John M. Jones, Abner Perrin, Leroy Stafford, and Junius Daniel.
8. Richard Anderson's.
9. On the lawn near the building where Stonewall Jackson had died.
10. James Longstreet.
11. Junius Daniel.
12. George Pickett. The reason was that these Confederates had joined the Union army.
13. From a carriage. The combination of diarrhea and heart disease had made him ill.
14. President Jefferson Davis.
15. William Mahone's.
16. Battle of the Wilderness.
17. Micah Jenkins. The bullet entered his brain.
18. Ambrose P. Hill.
19. Seth Barton.
20. Jubal Early.
21. Richard Anderson.
22. Major General Franz Sigel at New Market.
23. David Hunter.
24. Jubal Early.
25. James Kemper.
26. Jubal Early.
27. The home of Francis Blair in Maryland.

28. Whose horse fell on him during the Battle of Cold Harbor, injuring his right leg?
29. Who was mortally wounded by Union Private John A. Huff?
30. Who was wearing a white flower when he was mortally wounded at Cedar Creek?
31. How many field armies did Robert E. Lee command?
32. Which general surrendered to Colonel James A. Beaver of the 148th Pennsylvania?
33. Who returned to the Army of Northern Virginia the day after the Battle of Cedar Creek?
34. Who was called the "Savior of the Valley"?
35. Whom did Joseph Anderson meet in Richmond on April 4, 1865?
36. Who was captured in a hospital in Petersburg on April 2, 1865?
37. Whose mother's home was the scene of one of the last Confederate cabinet meetings?
38. Who covered Lee's withdrawal from Richmond?
39. Who was wounded at Yellow Tavern?
40. Who was captured in the hospital at Petersburg?
41. On January 23, 1865 President Jefferson Davis signed a bill for appointing a general in chief. Whom did he put in this position?
42. With whom did James Longstreet meet on February 21, 1865, to talk about ending the war?
43. When Richmond fell, who was instrumental in saving many of the military records?

28. John Breckinridge's.
29. Jeb Stuart.
30. Stephen Ramseur. The reason was to honor the birth of the child he would never see.
31. Just one. That is until the last two months of the war when he was given the title of general in chief.
32. "Maryland" Steuart.
33. James Longstreet.
34. Thomas Rosser.
35. President Abraham Lincoln.
36. Philip Cook.
37. Martin Gary's mother's home at Cokesbury.
38. Rufus Barringer.
39. Jeb Stuart.
40. Philip Cook.
41. Robert E. Lee.
42. Major General O.C. Ord.
43. John C. Breckinridge.

Appomattox

1. Who advised dispersing the army and carrying on a guerilla war?
2. Who were the eight generals captured at Sailor's Creek?
3. Did Robert E. Lee write any battle reports for 1864 and 1865?
4. How many men had fought as major generals under Robert E. Lee?
5. Which three lieutenant generals commanded on the Richmond-Petersburg line?
6. How many men had fought as brigadier generals under Robert E. Lee?
7. Who drew the last line of battle at Appomattox?
8. To whom did Robert E. Lee assign the job of arranging the details of the surrender?
9. Who commanded one of the last attacks at Appomattox on April 9, 1865?
10. Whose brigade fired the last volley at Appomattox?
11. Who was relieved of duty the day before the surrender?
12. On what date did Lee surrender to Grant?
13. Who was the only staff officer to go with Lee to meet Grant?
14. Which lieutenant general was with Lee on April 9, 1865?
15. Who rode at the front of the Confederate column at the surrender ceremonies at Appomattox?
16. Who surrendered the largest brigade in the army at Appomattox?
17. At whose home did Robert E. Lee surrender to Ulysses S. Grant?
18. Who refused to surrender with Lee?
19. Who was buried wearing the coat that he had worn during the surrender at Appomattox?

✎Appomattox (answers)

1. Edward Porter Alexander.
2. Richard Ewell, Joseph Kershaw, Custis Lee, Montgomery Corse, Dudley DuBose, Eppa Hunton, Seth Barton, and James Simms.
3. No. The wagons with the records were burned on the way to Appomattox.
4. 47. When the retreat from Petersburg began there were 13. At Appomattox there were seven.
5. James Longstreet, Richard Ewell, and Richard Anderson.
6. 146. There were 22 left at the surrender.
7. Edward Porter Alexander.
8. James Longstreet, John Gordon, and William Pendleton.
9. Bryan Grimes.
10. William Cox's.
11. Richard Anderson, George Pickett, and Bushrod Johnson. The reason was they had no command.
12. Palm Sunday, April 9, 1865.
13. Charles Marshall.
14. James Longstreet.
15. John Gordon.
16. John Bratton.
17. Wilmer McLean's.
18. Major General Lunsford Lomax.
19. George T. Anderson.

Appendix

The Generals

Edward Porter Alexander
Born: May 26, 1835, in Washington, Georgia.
Education: Graduated from West Point in 1857. He was third in his class.
Brigadier General: March 1, 1864, to rank from February 26, 1864.
Died: April 28, 1910, in Savannah, Georgia.
Buried: City Cemetery (Magnolia Cemetery) in Augusta, Georgia.

George Burgwyn Anderson
Born: April 12, 1831, in Hillsborough, North Carolina.
Education: Graduated from West Point in 1852. He was 10th in his class.
Brigadier General: June 9, 1862, to rank immediately.
Died: October 16, 1862, in Raleigh, North Carolina.
Buried: At the Oakwood Cemetery in Raleigh, North Carolina.

George Thomas Anderson
Born: February 3, 1824, at Covington, Georgia.
Education: Emory College. Left to join the Mexican War.
Brigadier General: November 1, 1862, to rank from the same date.
Died: April 4, 1901, at Anniston, Alabama.
Buried: Edgemont Cemetery in Anniston, Alabama.

Joseph Reid Anderson
Born: February 16, 1813, in Botetourt County, Virginia.
Education: Graduated from West Point in 1836. He ranked fourth in his class.
Brigadier General: September 3, 1861, to rank from the same date. He resigned on July 19, 1862.
Died: September 7, 1892, in Shoals, New Hampshire.
Buried: Hollywood Cemetery in Richmond, Virginia.

Richard Heron Anderson
    Born: October 7, 1821, in Sumter County, South Carolina.
    Education: Graduated 40th in his class at West Point in 1842.
    Brigadier General: July 17, 1861, to rank from the same date.
    Major General: July 14, 1862.
    Lieutenant General: June 1, 1864, to rank from May 31, 1864.
    Died: June 26, 1879, in Beaufort, South Carolina.
    Buried: St. Helena's Episcopal Church in Beaufort, South Carolina.

Samuel Read Anderson
    Born: February 17, 1804, in Bedford County, Virginia.
    Brigadier General: July 9, 1861, to rank immediately. Resigned spring
        1861 due to ill health.
    Died: January 2, 1883, in Nashville, Tennessee.
    Buried: Old City Cemetery in Nashville, Tennessee.

James Jay Archer
    Born: December 19, 1817, in Bel Air, Maryland.
    Education: Graduated from Princeton University in 1835. He then stud-
        ied law at the University of Maryland.
    Brigadier General: June 3, 1862, to rank from the same date.
    Died: October 24, 1864, in Richmond, Virginia.
    Buried: Hollywood Cemetery in Richmond, Virginia.

Lewis Addison Armistead
    Born: February 18, 1817, in New Berne, North Carolina.
    Education: He was dismissed from West Point in 1836.
    Brigadier General: April 1, 1862, to rank from the same date.
    Died: July 5, 1863, in a field hospital in Gettysburg, Pennsylvania. He
        had been mortally wounded on July 3.
    Buried: St. Paul's Churchyard in Baltimore, Maryland.

Laurence Simmons Baker
    Born: May 15, 1830, in Gates County, North Carolina.
    Education: Graduated 42nd in his class at West Point in 1851.
    Brigadier General: July 30, 1863, to rank from July 23, 1863.
    Died: April 10, 1907, in Suffolk, Virginia.
    Buried: Cedar Hill Cemetery in Suffolk, Virginia.

William Barksdale
    Born: August 21, 1821, in Rutherford County, Tennessee.
    Education: University of Nashville.
    Brigadier General: August 12, 1862, to rank from the same date.
    Died: Mortally wounded at Gettysburg on July 2, 1863. He died on July 3.
    Buried: Greenwood Cemetery in Jackson, Mississippi.

Rufus Barringer
Born: December 2, 1821, at "Poplar Grove" in Cabarrus County, North Carolina.
Education: Graduated from the University of North Carolina in 1842. He then studied law.
Brigadier General: June 1, 1864, to rank from the same date.
Died: February 3, 1895, at Poplar Grove, North Carolina.
Buried: Elmwood Cemetery near Charlotte, North Carolina.

John Decatur Barry
Born: June 21, 1839, in Wilmington, North Carolina.
Education: University of North Carolina.
Brigadier General: August 8, 1864, to rank from August 3, 1864.
Died: March 24, 1867, in Wilmington, North Carolina.
Buried: Oakdale Cemetery in Wilmington, North Carolina.

Seth Maxwell Barton
Born: September 8, 1829, in Fredericksburg, Virginia.
Education: Graduated from West Point in the lower half of his class in 1849.
Brigadier General: March 18, 1862, to rank from March 11, 1862.
Died: April 11, 1900, at Fredericksburg, Virginia.
Buried: City Cemetery (Confederate Cemetery) in Fredericksburg, Virginia.

Cullen Andrews Battle
Born: June 1, 1829, in Powelton, Georgia.
Education: State University of Alabama.
Brigadier General: August 25, 1863, to rank from August 20, 1863.
Died: April 8, 1905, in Greensborough, North Carolina.
Buried: Blandford Cemetery in Petersburg, Virginia.

Richard Lee Turberville Beale
Born: May 22, 1819, at "Hickory Hill" in Westmoreland County, Virginia.
Education: Dickinson College and the University of Virginia. Admitted to the bar in 1837.
Brigadier General: January 13, 1865, to rank from January 6, 1865.
Died: April 21, 1893, in Hague, Virginia.
Buried: Hickory Hill Cemetery in Hague, Virginia.

Henry Lewis Benning
Born: April 2, 1814, in Columbia County, Georgia.
Education: Graduated from Franklin College (now the University of Georgia) in 1834.
Brigadier General: April 23, 1863, to rank from January 17, 1863.
Died: July 10, 1875, in Columbus, Georgia.
Buried: Linwood Cemetery in Columbus, Georgia.

Lawrence O'Bryan Branch
Born: November 28, 1820, in Enfield, North Carolina.
Education: Graduated from Princeton in 1838.
Brigadier General: November 16, 1861, to rank from the same date.
Died: September 17, 1862. He was killed by a Federal sharpshooter during the Battle of Antietam.
Buried: Old City Cemetery in Raleigh, North Carolina.

John Bratton
Born: March 7, 1831, in Winnsboro, South Carolina.
Education: He attended Mount Zion Academy. He graduated from South Carolina College in 1853 with a degree in medicine.
Brigadier General: June 9, 1864, to rank from May 6, 1864.
Died: January 12, 1898, in Winnsboro, South Carolina.
Buried: St. John's Episcopal Church Cemetery in Winnsboro, South Carolina.

John Cabell Breckinridge
Born: January 15, 1821, in Lexington, Kentucky.
Education: He graduated from Centre College in 1839. He then studied law at Transylvania College.
Brigadier General: November 2, 1861, to rank from the same date.
Major General: April 18, 1862, to rank from April 14, 1862.
Died: May 17, 1875, in Lexington, Kentucky.
Buried: City Cemetery in Lexington, Kentucky.

Theodore Washington Brevard
Born: August 26, 1835, in Tuskegee, Alabama.
Education: Attended the University of Virginia.
Brigadier General: March 28, 1865, to rank from March 22, 1865.
Died: June 20, 1882, in Tallahassee, Florida.
Buried: Episcopal Cemetery in Tallahassee, Florida.

Goode Bryan
Born: August 31, 1811, in Hancock County, Georgia.
Education: Graduated 25th in his class at West Point in 1834.
Brigadier General: August 31, 1863, to rank from August 29, 1863.
Died: August 16, 1885, in Augusta, Georgia.
Buried: City Cemetery (Magnolia Cemetery) in Augusta, Georgia.

Matthew Calbraith Butler
Born: March 8, 1836, in Greenville, South Carolina.
Education: South Carolina College.
Brigadier General: September 1, 1863, to rank from the same date.
Major General: December 7, 1864, to rank from September 19, 1864.
Died: April 14, 1909, in Washington, D.C.
Buried: Willow Brook Cemetery in Edgefield, South Carolina.

John Randolph Chambliss, Jr.
Born: January 23, 1833, at Hicksford in Greenville County, Virginia.
Education: Graduated 31st in his class at West Point in 1853.
Brigadier General: January 27, 1864, to rank from December 19, 1863.
Died: August 16, 1864, after being wounded outside of Richmond, Virginia.
Buried: Family cemetery at Emporia, Virginia.

Robert Hall Chilton
Born: February 25, 1815, in Loudoun County, Virginia.
Education: Graduated 48th in his class at West Point in 1837.
Brigadier General: February 16, 1864, to rank from December 21, 1863.
Died: February 18, 1879, in Columbus, Georgia.
Buried: Hollywood Cemetery in Richmond, Virginia.

Thomas Lanier Clingman
Born: July 27, 1812, in Huntersville, North Carolina.
Brigadier General: May 17, 1862, to rank from the same date.
Died: November 3, 1897, in Morgantown, North Carolina.
Buried: Riverside Cemetery in Asheville, North Carolina.

Howell Cobb
Born: September 7, 1815, at "Cherry Hill" in Jefferson County, Georgia.
Education: Graduated from the University of Georgia in 1834.
Brigadier General: February 12, 1862, to rank from the same date.
Major General: September 19, 1863, to rank from September 4, 1863.
Died: October 9, 1868, in New York City.
Buried: Oconee Hill Cemetery in Athens, Georgia.

Thomas Reade Rootes Cobb
Born: April 10, 1823, at "Cherry Hill" in Jefferson County, Georgia.
Education: Attended the University of Georgia.
Brigadier General: November 1, 1862, to rank from the same date.
Died: He bled to death in a house on the battlefield at Fredericksburg on
    December 13, 1862.
Buried: Oconee Hill Cemetery in Athens, Georgia.

Philip St. George Cocke
Born: April 17, 1809, at "Bremo Bluff" in Fluvanna County, Virginia.
Education: Graduated sixth in his class at West Point in 1832.
Brigadier General: October 21, 1861, to rank from the same date.
Died: He committed suicide on December 26, 1861.
Buried: Hollywood Cemetery in Richmond, Virginia.

Alfred Holt Colquitt

Born: April 20, 1824, in Walton County, Georgia.
Education: Graduated from Princeton University in 1844.
Brigadier General: September 1, 1862, to rank from the same date.
Died: March 26, 1894, in Washington, D.C.
Buried: Rose Hill Cemetery in Macon, Georgia.

Raleigh Edward Colston

Born: October 31, 1825, in Paris, France.
Education: Graduated from the Virginia Military Institute in 1846.
Brigadier General: December 24, 1861, to rank from the same date.
Died: July 29, 1896, in Richmond, Virginia.
Buried: Hollywood Cemetery in Richmond, Virginia.

James Conner

Born: September 1, 1829, in Charleston, South Carolina.
Education: Attended South Carolina College.
Brigadier General: June 1, 1864, to rank from the same date.
Died: June 26, 1883, in Richmond, Virginia.
Buried: Magnolia Cemetery in Charleston, South Carolina.

Philip Cook

Born: July 31, 1817, in Twiggs County, Georgia.
Education: Attended Oglethorpe University. Graduated from the University of Virginia Law School in 1841.
Brigadier General: August 8, 1864, to rank from August 5, 1864.
Died: May 21, 1894, in Atlanta, Georgia.
Buried: Rose Hill Cemetery in Macon, Georgia.

John Rogers Cooke

Born: June 9, 1833, in Jefferson Barracks, Maryland.
Education: Attended Harvard University.
Brigadier General: November 1, 1862, to rank from the same date.
Died: April 10, 1891, in Richmond, Virginia.
Buried: Hollywood Cemetery in Richmond, Virginia.

Montgomery Dent Corse

Born: March 14, 1816, in Alexandria, Virginia.
Brigadier General: November 1, 1862, to rank from the same date.
Died: February 11, 1895, in Alexandria, Virginia.
Buried: St. Paul's Cemetery in Alexandria, Virginia.

William Ruffin Cox
  Born: March 11, 1832, at "Scotland Neck" in Halifax County, North Carolina.
  Brigadier General: June 2, 1864, to rank from May 31, 1864.
  Died: December 26, 1919, in Richmond, Virginia.
  Buried: Oakwood Cemetery in Raleigh, North Carolina.

Alfred Cumming
  Born: January 30, 1829, in Augusta, Georgia.
  Education: Graduated 35th in his class at West Point in 1849.
  Brigadier General: October 19, 1862, to rank from the same date.
  Died: December 5, 1910, in Rome, Georgia.
  Buried: Summerville Cemetery at Augusta, Georgia.

Junius Daniel
  Born: June 27, 1828, in Halifax, North Carolina.
  Education: Graduated 33rd in his class at West Point in 1851.
  Brigadier General: September 20, 1862, to rank from September 1, 1862.
  Died: May 13, 1864, after being mortally wounded during the Battle of
      Spotsylvania on May 12, 1864.
  Buried: Old Colonial Churchyard Cemetery in Halifax, North Carolina.

Joseph Robert Davis
  Born: January 12, 1825, in Woodville, Mississippi.
  Education: Attended Miami University.
  Brigadier General: October 8, 1862, to rank from September 15, 1862.
  Died: September 15, 1896, in Biloxi, Mississippi.
  Buried: Biloxi Cemetery in Biloxi, Mississippi.

James Dearing
  Born: April 25, 1840, at "Otterburne" in Campbell County, Virginia.
  Brigadier General: April 29, 1864. There is no record of his promotion.
  Died: April 23, 1865, at Lynchburg, Virginia. He had been mortally
      wounded on April 6, 1865.
  Buried: Spring Hill Cemetery in Lynchburg, Virginia.

George Pierce Doles
  Born: May 14, 1830, in Milledgeville, Georgia.
  Brigadier General: November 1, 1862, to rank from the same date.
  Died: Killed on June 2, 1864, by a Federal sharpshooter.
  Buried: Memory Hill Cemetery in Milledgeville, Georgia.

Thomas Fenwick Drayton
Born: August 24, 1808, in Charleston, South Carolina.
Education: Graduated 28th in his class at West Point in 1828.
Brigadier General: September 25, 1861, to rank from the same date.
Died: February 18, 1891, at Florence, South Carolina.
Buried: Elmwood Cemetery in Charlotte, North Carolina.

Dudley McIver DuBose
Born: October 28, 1834, in Shelby County, Tennessee.
Education: Attended the University of Mississippi and the Lebanon Law School.
Brigadier General: December 15, 1864, to rank from November 16, 1864.
Died: March 2, 1883, at Washington, Georgia.
Buried: Rest Haven Cemetery in Washington, Georgia.

John Dunovant
Born: March 5, 1825, in Chester, South Carolina.
Brigadier General: August 22, 1864, to rank from the same date.
Died: Killed on the Vaughan Road on October 1, 1864.
Buried: Family plot three miles from Chester, South Carolina.

Jubal Anderson Early
Born: November 3, 1816, in Franklin County, Virginia.
Education: Graduated 18th in his class at West Point in 1837.
Brigadier General: August 28, 1861, to rank from July 21, 1861.
Major General: April 23, 1863, to rank from January 17, 1863.
Lieutenant General: May 31, 1864, to rank from the same date.
Died: March 2, 1894, at Lynchburg, Virginia.
Buried: Spring Hill Cemetery at Lynchburg, Virginia.

John Echols
Born: March 20, 1823, in Lynchburg, Virginia.
Education: Attended Washington College and Harvard University.
Brigadier General: April 18, 1862, to rank from April 16, 1862.
Died: May 24, 1896, in Staunton, Virginia.
Buried: Thornrose Cemetery in Staunton, Virginia.

Stephen Elliott, Jr.
Born: October 26, 1830, in Beaufort, South Carolina.
Education: Attended Harvard University, and South Carolina College.
Brigadier General: May 28, 1864, to rank from May 24, 1864.
Died: February 21, 1866, at Aiken, South Carolina.
Buried: St. Helena's Episcopal Churchyard in Beaufort, South Carolina.

Arnold Elzey

Born: December 18, 1816, at "Elmwood" in Somerset County, Maryland.
Education: Graduated from West Point in 1837.
Brigadier General: August 28, 1861, to rank from July 21,1861.
Major General: December 4, 1862.
Died: February 21, 1871, in Baltimore, Maryland.
Buried: Green Mount Cemetery in Baltimore, Maryland.

Clement Anselm Evans

Born: February 25, 1833, in Stewart County, Georgia.
Brigadier General: May 20, 1864, to rank from May 19, 1864.
Died: July 2, 1911, in Atlanta, Georgia.
Buried: Oakland Cemetery in Atlanta, Georgia.

Nathan George Evans

Born: February 3, 1824, in Marion, South Carolina.
Education: Attended Randolph-Macon College. Graduated from West Point in 1848.
Brigadier General: October 21, 1861, to rank from the same date.
Died: November 23, 1868, in Midway, Alabama.
Buried: Tabernacle Cemetery in Cokesbury, South Carolina.

Richard Stoddert Ewell

Born: February 8, 1817, in Georgetown.
Education: Graduated 13th in a class of 42 from West Point in 1840.
Brigadier General: June 17, 1861, to rank from the same date.
Major General: January 24, 1862, to rank from the same date.
Lieutenant General: May 23, 1863, to rank from the same date.
Died: January 25, 1872, near Spring Hill, Tennessee.
Buried: Old City Cemetery in Nashville, Tennessee.

Winfield Scott Featherston

Born: August 8, 1820, near Murfreesboro, Tennessee.
Brigadier General: March 6, 1862, to rank from March 4, 1862.
Died: May 28, 1891, in Holly Springs, Mississippi.
Buried: Hillcrest Cemetery in Holly Springs, Mississippi.

Charles William Field

Born: April 6, 1828, at "Mount Airy" in Woodford County, Kentucky.
Education: Graduated from West Point in 1849.
Brigadier General: March 14, 1862, to rank from March 9, 1862.
Major General: February 12, 1864, to rank from the same date.
Died: April 9, 1892, in Washington, D.C.
Buried: London Park Cemetery in Baltimore, Maryland.

William Henry Forney
Born: November 9, 1823, in Lincolnton, North Carolina.
Education: Graduated from State University in Alabama in 1844.
Brigadier General: February 23, 1865, to rank from February 15, 1865.
Died: January 16, 1894, in Jacksonville, Alabama.
Buried: City Cemetery in Jacksonville, Alabama.

Birkett Davenport Fry
Born: June 24, 1822, in Kanawha County, (West) Virginia.
Education: Attended the Virginia Military Institute.
Brigadier General: May 24, 1861, to rank from the same date.
Died: January 21, 1891, in Richmond, Virginia.
Buried: Oakwood Cemetery in Montgomery, Alabama.

Samuel Garland, Jr.
Born: December 16, 1830, in Lynchburg, Virginia.
Education: Attended the Virginia Military Institute. He studied law at the University of Virginia.
Brigadier General: May 23, 1862, to rank from the same date.
Died: Killed September 14, 1862, at the Battle of South Mountain.
Buried: Presbyterian Cemetery in Lynchburg, Virginia.

Richard Brooke Garnett
Born: November 21, 1817, at "Rose Hill" in Essex County, Virginia.
Education: Graduated from West Point in 1841.
Brigadier General: November 14, 1861, to rank from the same date.
Died: July 3, 1863, at Gettysburg, Pennsylvania.
Buried: His body was never found after the battle. He has a marker in Hollywood Cemetery in Richmond, Virginia.

Martin Witherspoon Gary
Born: March 25, 1831, in Cokesbury, South Carolina.
Education: Graduated from Harvard in 1854.
Brigadier General: June 14, 1861, to rank from May 18, 1864.
Died: April 9, 1881, in Edgefield County, South Carolina.
Buried: Tabernacle Cemetery in Cokesbury, South Carolina.

Archibald Campbell Godwin
Born: 1831 in Nansemond County, Virginia.
Brigadier General: August 9, 1864, to rank from August 5, 1864.
Died: Killed on September 19, 1864, in Winchester, Virginia.
Buried: Stonewall Cemetery in Winchester, Virginia.

James Monroe Goggin
Born: October 23, 1820, in Bedford County, Virginia.
Brigadier General: December 4, 1864, to rank from the same date.
Died: October 10, 1889, in Austin, Texas.
Buried: Oakwood Cemetery in Austin, Texas.

James Byron Gordon
Born: November 2, 1822, in Wilkesboro, North Carolina.
Education: Attended Emory and Henry College.
Brigadier General: September 28, 1863, to rank from the same date.
Died: May 18, 1864, in Richmond, Virginia.
Buried: St. Paul's Episcopal Church Cemetery in Wilkesboro, North Carolina.

John Brown Gordon
Born: February 6, 1832, in Upson County, Georgia.
Brigadier General: November 1, 1862, to rank from the same date.
Major General: May 14, 1864, to rank from the same date.
Died: January 9, 1904, in Miami, Florida.
Buried: Oakland Cemetery in Atlanta, Georgia.

John Gregg
Born: September 28, 1828, in Lawrence County, Alabama.
Education: Attended Louisiana Grange College.
Brigadier General: September 27, 1862, to rank from August 29, 1862.
Died: Killed outside of Richmond on October 7, 1864.
Buried: Odd Fellows Cemetery in Aberdeen, Mississippi.

Maxcy Gregg
Born: August 1, 1814, in Columbia, South Carolina.
Education: Attended South Carolina College.
Brigadier General: December 14, 1861, to rank from the same date.
Died: December 15, 1862, in Fredericksburg, Virginia.
Buried: Elmwood Cemetery in Columbia, South Carolina.

Richard Griffith
Born: January 11, 1814, near Philadelphia, Pennsylvania.
Education: Attended Ohio University.
Brigadier General: November 2, 1861, to rank from the same date.
Died: June 29, 1862, at the Battle of Savage's Station, Virginia.
Buried: Greenwood Cemetery in Jackson, Mississippi.

Bryan Grimes
Born: November 2, 1828, at "Grimesland" in Pitt County, North Carolina.
Education: Attended University of North Carolina.
Brigadier General: June 1, 1864, to rank from May 19, 1864.
Major General: February 23, 1865, to rank from February 15, 1865.
Died: August 14, 1880, at his plantation in North Carolina.
Buried: Trinity Churchyard in Pitt City, North Carolina.

Johnson Hagood
Born: February 21, 1829, in Barnwell County, South Carolina.
Education: Attended South Carolina Military Academy.
Brigadier General: July 21, 1862, to rank from the same date.
Died: January 4, 1898, in Barnwell County, South Carolina.
Buried: Episcopal Churchyard in Barnwell, South Carolina.

Wade Hampton
Born: March 28, 1818, in Charleston, South Carolina.
Education: Attended South Carolina College.
Brigadier General: May 23, 1862, to rank from the same date.
Major General: September 3, 1863, to rank from August 3, 1863.
Lieutenant General: February 15, 1865, to rank from February 14, 1865.
Died: April 11, 1902, at Columbia, South Carolina.
Buried: Trinity Episcopal Church Cemetery in Columbia, South Carolina.

Nathaniel Harrison Harris
Born: August 22, 1834, in Natchez, Mississippi.
Education: Attended the University of Louisiana (Tulane).
Brigadier General: February 17, 1864, to rank from January 20, 1864.
Died: August 23, 1900, in Malvern, England.
Buried: Cremated and interred in the Greenwood Cemetery in Brooklyn, New York.

Harry Thompson Hays
Born: April 14, 1820, in Wilson County, Tennessee.
Education: Attended St. Mary's College.
Brigadier General: July 25, 1862, to rank from the same date.
Died: August 21, 1876, in New Orleans, Louisiana.
Buried: Washington Avenue Cemetery (Lafayette Cemetery No. 1) in New Orleans, Louisiana.

Henry Heth
Born: December 16, 1825, in Chesterfield County, Virginia.
Education: Graduated 38th in a class of 38 from West Point in 1847.
Brigadier General: January 6, 1862, to rank from the same date.
Major General: May 23, 1863, to rank from May 22, 1863.
Died: September 27, 1899, in Washington, D.C.
Buried: Hollywood Cemetery in Richmond, Virginia.

Ambrose Powell Hill

Born: November 9, 1825, in Culpeper, Virginia.
Education: Graduated from West Point in 1847.
Brigadier General: February 26, 1862, to rank from the same date.
Major General: May 26, 1862, to rank from the same date.
Lieutenant General: May 24, 1863, to rank from the same date.
Died: April 2, 1865, after being shot by a Federal trooper.
Buried: He is buried under his monument in Richmond, Virginia. The monument is located at the intersection of Laburnum and Hermitage Avenues.

Daniel Harvey Hill

Born: July 12, 1821, in the York District, South Carolina.
Education: Graduated 28th in his class at West Point in 1842.
Brigadier General: July 10, 1861, to rank from the same date.
Major General: March 26, 1862, to rank from the same date.
Lieutenant General: July 11, 1863, to rank from the same date.
Died: September 24, 1889, in Charlotte, North Carolina.
Buried: Davidson College Cemetery in Davidson, North Carolina.

Robert Frederick Hoke

Born: May 27, 1837, in Lincolnton, North Carolina.
Education: Attended the Kentucky Military Institute.
Brigadier General: April 23, 1863, to rank from January 17, 1863.
Major General: April 23, 1864, to rank from April 20, 1864.
Died: July 3, 1912, at Raleigh, North Carolina.
Buried: Oakwood Cemetery in Raleigh, North Carolina.

Theophilus Hunter Holmes

Born: November 13, 1804, in Sampson County, North Carolina.
Education: Graduated 44th in a class of 46 from West Point in 1829.
Brigadier General: June 5, 1861, to rank from the same date.
Major General: October 7, 1861, to rank from the same date.
Lieutenant General: October 10, 1862, to rank from the same date.
Died: June 21, 1880, in Fayetteville, North Carolina.
Buried: MacPherson Presbyterian Church Cemetery in Fayetteville, North Carolina.

John Bell Hood

Born: June 1, 1831, in Owingsville, Kentucky.
Education: Graduated 44th in a class of 52 from West Point in 1853.
Brigadier General: March 6, 1862, to rank from March 3, 1862.
Major General: October 11, 1862, to rank from October 10, 1862.
Lieutenant General: February 1, 1864, to rank from September 20, 1863.
General: July 18, 1864, to rank from the same date.
Died: August 30, 1879, in New Orleans, Louisiana.
Buried: Metaire Cemetery in New Orleans, Louisiana.

Benjamin Huger
Born: November 22, 1805, in Charleston, South Carolina.
Education: Graduated 8th in a class of 37 from West Point in 1825.
Brigadier General: June 17, 1861, to rank from the same date.
Major General: October 7, 1861, to rank from the same date.
Died: December 7, 1877, in Charleston, South Carolina.
Buried: Green Mount Cemetery in Baltimore, Maryland.

Benjamin Grubb Humphreys
Born: August 24, 1808, in Clairborne County, Mississippi.
Brigadier General: August 14, 1863, to rank from August 12, 1863.
Died: December 20, 1882, in Leflore County, Mississippi at his plantation.
Buried: Winter Green Cemetery in Port Gibson, Mississippi.

Eppa Hunton
Born: September 22, 1822, in Fauquier County, Virginia.
Brigadier General: August 12, 1863, to rank from August 9, 1863.
Died: October 11, 1908, in Richmond, Virginia.
Buried: Hollywood Cemetery in Richmond, Virginia.

John Daniel Imboden
Born: February 16, 1823, near Staunton, Virginia.
Education: Attended Washington College.
Brigadier General: April 13, 1863, to rank from January 28, 1863.
Died: August 15, 1895, in Damascus, Virginia.
Buried: Hollywood Cemetery in Richmond, Virginia.

Alfred Iverson, Jr.
Born: February 14, 1829, in Clinton, Georgia.
Brigadier General: November 1, 1862, to rank from the same date.
Died: March 31, 1911, in Atlanta, Georgia.
Buried: Oakland Cemetery in Atlanta, Georgia.

Thomas Jonathan Jackson
Born: January 21, 1824, in Clarksburg, (West) Virginia.
Education: Graduated 17th in the class of 1846 from West Point.
Brigadier General: June 17, 1861, to rank from the same date.
Major General: October 7, 1861, to rank from the same date.
Lieutenant General: October 11, 1862, to rank from October 10, 1862.
Died: May 10, 1863, at Guinea Station, Virginia.
Buried: Jackson Memorial Cemetery in Lexington, Virginia. His ampu-
tated arm is buried near the Chancellorsville Battlefield.

William Lowther Jackson
Born: February 3, 1825, in Clarksburg, (West) Virginia.
Brigadier General: December 19, 1864, to rank from the same date.
Died: March 24, 1890, in Louisville, Kentucky.
Buried: Cave Hill Cemetery in Louisville, Kentucky.

Albert Gallatin Jenkins

Born: November 10, 1830, in Cabell County, (West) Virginia.

Education: Jefferson College in Cannonsburg, Pennsylvania. He also attended the Harvard Law School.

Brigadier General: August 5, 1862, to rank from the same date.

Died: May 21, 1864, near Dublin, Virginia.

Buried: Spring Hill Cemetery in Huntington, West Virginia.

Micah Jenkins

Born: December 1, 1835, on Edisto Island, South Carolina.

Education: Graduated from the South Carolina Military Academy in 1854.

Brigadier General: July 22, 1862, to rank from the same date.

Died: May 6, 1864, during the Battle of the Wilderness.

Buried: Magnolia Cemetery in Charleston, South Carolina.

Bradley Tyler Johnson

Born: September 29, 1829, in Frederick, Maryland.

Education: Attended Princeton University.

Brigadier General: June 28, 1864, to rank from the same date.

Died: October 5, 1903, in Amelia, Virginia.

Buried: Loudon Park Cemetery in Baltimore, Maryland.

Bushrod Rust Johnson

Born: October 7, 1817, in Belmont County, Ohio.

Education: Graduated 23rd in a class of 42 from West Point in 1840.

Brigadier General: January 24, 1862, to rank from the same date.

Major General: May 26, 1864, to rank from May 21, 1864.

Died: September 12, 1880, near Brighton, Illinois.

Buried: Old City Cemetery in Nashville, Tennessee.

Edward Johnson

Born: April 16, 1816, at "Salisbury" near Midlothian, Virginia.

Education: Graduated 32nd in a class of 45 from West Point in 1838.

Brigadier General: December 13, 1861, to rank from the same date.

Major General: April 22, 1863, to rank from February 28, 1863.

Died: March 2, 1873, in Richmond, Virginia.

Buried: Hollywood Cemetery in Richmond, Virginia.

Robert Daniel Johnston

Born: March 19, 1837, in Lincoln County, North Carolina.

Education: Attended the University of North Carolina, and the University of Virginia.

Brigadier General: September 1, 1863, to rank from the same date.

Died: February 1, 1919, in Winchester, Virginia.

Buried: Winchester, Virginia.

David Rumph Jones
Born: April 5, 1825, in Orangeburg District, South Carolina.
Education: Graduated 41st in a class of 59 from West Point in 1846.
Brigadier General: June 17, 1861, to rank from the same date.
Major General: April 5, 1862, to rank from March 10, 1862.
Died: January 15, 1863, in Richmond, Virginia.
Buried: Hollywood Cemetery in Richmond, Virginia.

John Marshall Jones
Born: July 26, 1820, in Charlottesville, Virginia.
Education: Graduated 39th in a class of 42 at West Point in 1841.
Brigadier General: May 15, 1863, to rank from the same date.
Died: May 5, 1864, during the Battle of Spotsylvania.
Buried: Maplewood Cemetery in Charlottesville, Virginia.

John Robert Jones
Born: March 12, 1827, at Harrisonburg, Virginia.
Education: Attended the Virginia Military Institute. He graduated in 1848.
Brigadier General: June 25, 1862, to rank from June 23, 1862.
Died: April 1, 1901, at Harrisonburg, Virginia.
Buried: Woodbine Cemetery in Harrisonburg, Virginia.

William Edmondson Jones
Born: May 9, 1824, in Washington County, Virginia.
Education: Attended Emory and Henry College. He graduated from West Point in 1848. He ranked 10th in a class of 38.
Brigadier General: October 3, 1862, to rank from September 19, 1862.
Died: June 5, 1864, during the Battle of Piedmont.
Buried: Old Glade Spring Presbyterian Church in Washington County, Virginia.

James Lawson Kemper
Born: June 11, 1823, at "Madison Prospect" in Madison County, Virginia.
Education: Graduated from Washington College in 1842.
Brigadier General: June 3, 1862, to rank from the same date.
Major General: September 19, 1864, to rank from the same date.
Died: April 7, 1895, at his plantation in Orange County, Virginia.
Buried: Family cemetery at his plantation.

Joseph Brevard Kershaw
Born: January 5, 1822, in Camden, South Carolina.
Brigadier General: February 15, 1862, to rank from February 13, 1862.
Major General: May 18, 1864, to rank from the same date.
Died: April 13, 1894, in Camden, South Carolina.
Buried: Quaker Cemetery in Camden, South Carolina.

William Whedbee Kirkland

Born: February 13, 1833, at "Ayrmont" in Hillsboro, North Carolina.

Brigadier General: August 31, 1863, to rank from August 29, 1863.

Died: May 12, 1915, in Washington, D.C.

Buried: Elmwood Cemetery in Shepherdstown, West Virginia.

James Henry Lane

Born: July 28, 1833, at Mathews Court House, Virginia.

Education: Graduated from the Virginia Military Institute in 1854. Graduated from the University of Virginia in 1857.

Brigadier General: November 1, 1862, to rank from the same date.

Died: September 21, 1907, at Auburn.

Buried: Pine Hill Cemetery in Auburn, Alabama.

Evander McIvor Law

Born: August 7, 1836, at Darlington, South Carolina.

Education: Graduated from South Carolina Military Academy in 1856.

Brigadier General: October 15, 1862, to rank from October 2, 1862.

Major General: March 20, 1865, to rank from the same date.

Died: October 31, 1920, at Bartow, Florida.

Buried: Oakhill Cemetery at Bartow, Florida.

Alexander Robert Lawton

Born: November 14, 1818, near Beaufort, South Carolina.

Education: Graduated from West Point in 1839. Graduated from Harvard Law School in 1842.

Brigadier General: February 17, 1861, to rank from the same date.

Died: July 2, 1896, at Clifton Springs, New York.

Buried: Bonaventure Cemetery in Savannah, Georgia.

Fitzhugh Lee

Born: November 19, 1835, at "Clermont" in Alexandria, Virginia.

Education: Graduated 45th in a class of 49 from West Point in 1856.

Brigadier General: July 24, 1862, to rank from the same date.

Major General: August 3, 1863, to rank from the same date.

Died: April 28, 1905, in Washington, D.C.

Buried: Hollywood Cemetery in Richmond, Virginia.

George Washington Custis Lee

Born: September 16, 1832, at Fort Monroe, Virginia.

Education: Graduated first in his class at West Point in 1854.

Brigadier General: June 25, 1863, to rank from the same date.

Major General: October 20, 1864, to rank from the same date.

Died: February 18, 1913, at "Ravensworth" near Alexandria, Virginia.

Buried: Lee Chapel in Lexington, Virginia.

Robert Edward Lee
Born: January 19, 1807, at "Stratford" in Westmoreland County, Virginia.
Education: Graduated second of 45 from West Point in 1829.
Brigadier General: May 14, 1861, to rank from the same date.
Major General: June 14, 1861, to rank from the same date.
Died: October 12, 1870, in Lexington, Virginia.
Buried: Lee Chapel in Lexington, Virginia.

Stephen Lee
Born: September 22, 1833, in Charleston, South Carolina.
Education: Graduated 17th in a class of 46 at West Point in 1854.
Brigadier General: November 6, 1862, to rank from the same date.
Major General: August 3, 1863, to rank from the same date.
Lieutenant General: March 16, 1865, to rank from June 23, 1864.
Died: May 28, 1908, in Vicksburg, Mississippi.
Buried: Friendship Cemetery in Columbus, Mississippi.

William Henry Fitzhugh Lee
Born: May 31, 1837, at "Arlington" near Alexandria, Virginia.
Education: Attended Harvard University.
Brigadier General: September 15, 1862, to rank from the same date.
Major General: April 23, 1864, to rank from the same date.
Died: October 15, 1891, near Alexandria, Virginia.
Buried: Alexandria, Virginia. In 1922 his body was moved to the Lee Chapel in Lexington, Virginia.

William Gaston Lewis
Born: September 3, 1835, in Rocky Mount, North Carolina.
Education: Attended the University of North Carolina.
Brigadier General: June 2, 1864, to rank from May 31, 1864.
Died: January 7, 1901, at Goldsboro, North Carolina.
Buried: Willow Dale Cemetery at Goldsboro, North Carolina.

Robert Doak Lilley
Born: January 28, 1836, near Greenville, Virginia.
Education: Attended Washington College.
Brigadier General: May 31, 1864, to rank from the same date.
Died: November 12, 1886, in Richmond, Virginia.
Buried: Thornrose Cemetery at Staunton, Virginia.

Lunsford Lindsay Lomax
Born: November 4, 1835, in Newport, Rhode Island.
Education: Graduated from West Point in 1856.
Brigadier General: July 30, 1863, to rank from July 23, 1863.
Major General: August 10, 1864, to rank from the same date.
Died: May 28, 1913, in Washington, D.C.
Buried: City Cemetery in Warrenton, Virginia.

Armistead Lindsay Long
Born: September 3, 1825, in Campbell County, Virginia.
Education: Graduated from West Point in 1850. He ranked 17th in his class.
Brigadier General: September 21, 1863, to rank from the same date.
Died: April 29, 1891, in Charlottesville, Virginia.
Buried: Maplewood Cemetery in Charlottesville, Virginia.

James Longstreet
Born: January 8, 1821, in Edgefield District, South Carolina.
Education: Graduated from West Point in 1842. He was ranked 54th in a class of 62.
Brigadier General: June 17, 1861, to rank from the same date.
Major General: October 7, 1861, to rank from the same date.
Lieutenant General: October 9, 1862, to rank from the same date.
Died: January 2, 1904, in Gainesville, Georgia.
Buried: Alta Vista Cemetery in Gainesville, Georgia.

John McCausland
Born: September 13, 1836, in St. Louis, Missouri.
Education: Graduated from the Virginia Military Institute in 1857. He was first in his class. He later attended the University of Virginia.
Brigadier General: May 18, 1864, to rank from the same date.
Died: January 22, 1927, in Mason County, West Virginia.
Buried: McCausland Cemetery in Henderson, West Virginia.

William McComb
Born: November 21, 1828, in Mercer County, Pennsylvania.
Brigadier General: February 13, 1865, to rank from January 20, 1865.
Died: July 21, 1918, near Gordonsville.
Buried: Mechanicsville Cemetery in Boswells, Virginia.

Samuel McGowan
Born: October 9, 1819, in Laurens District, South Carolina.
Education: Attended South Carolina College.
Brigadier General: April 23, 1863, to rank from January 17, 1863.
Died: August 9, 1897, in Abbeville, South Carolina.
Buried: Long Cane Cemetery outside of Abbeville, South Carolina.

Lafayette McLaws
Born: January 15, 1821, in Augusta, Georgia.
Education: Graduated from West Point in 1842. He ranked 48th in a class of 56.
Brigadier General: September 25, 1861, to rank from the same date.
Major General: May 23, 1862, to rank from the same date.
Died: July 24, 1897, in Savannah, Georgia.
Buried: Laurel Grove Cemetery in Savannah, Georgia.

William MacRae
Born: September 9, 1834, in Wilmington, North Carolina.
Brigadier General: November 5, 1864, to rank from November 4, 1864.
Died: February 11, 1882, at Augusta, Georgia.
Buried: Oakdale Cemetery in Wilmington, North Carolina.

John Bankhead Magruder
Born: May 1, 1807, in Port Royal, Virginia.
Education: Graduated from West Point in 1830. He ranked 15th in a class of 42.
Brigadier General: June 17, 1861, to rank from the same date.
Major General: October 7, 1861, to rank from the same date.
Died: February 18, 1871, in Houston, Texas.
Buried: Episcopal Cemetery in Galveston, Texas.

William Mahone
Born: December 1, 1826, in Southampton County, Virginia.
Education: He graduated from the Virginia Military Institute in 1847.
Brigadier General: November 16, 1861, to rank from the same date.
Major General: August 3, 1864, to rank from July 30, 1864.
Died: October 8, 1895, in Washington, D.C.
Buried: Blandford Cemetery in Petersburg, Virginia.

William Thompson Martin
Born: March 25, 1823, in Glasgow, Kentucky.
Education: Attended Centre College, from which he graduated in 1840.
Brigadier General: December 2, 1862, to rank from the same date.
Major General: November 12, 1863, to rank from November 10, 1863.
Died: March 16, 1910, near Natchez, Mississippi.
Buried: City Cemetery in Natchez, Mississippi.

Young Marshall Moody
Born: June 23, 1822, in Chesterfield County, Virginia.
Brigadier General: March 13, 1865, to rank from March 4, 1865.
Died: September 18, 1866, in New Orleans, Louisiana.
Buried: Greenwood Cemetery in New Orleans, Louisiana.

Patrick Theodore Moore
Born: September 22, 1821, in Galway, Ireland.
Brigadier General: September 20, 1864, to rank from the same date.
Died: February 19, 1883, in Richmond, Virginia.
Buried: Shockoe Cemetery in Richmond, Virginia.

John Tyler Morgan
Born: June 20, 1824, in Athens, Tennessee.
Brigadier General: November 17, 1863, to rank from November 16, 1863.
Died: June 11, 1907, in Washington, D.C.
Buried: Live Oak Cemetery in Selma, Alabama.

Elisha Franklin Paxton
Born: March 4, 1828, in Rockbridge County, Virginia.
Education: Graduated from Washington College in 1845. Graduated from Yale University in 1847. He also attended the University of Virginia.
Brigadier General: November 1, 1862, to rank from the same date.
Died: May 3, 1863, after being hit by a minie ball through his chest.
Buried: Jackson Memorial Cemetery in Lexington, Virginia.

William Henry Fitzhugh Payne
Born: January 27, 1830, in Fauquier County, Virginia.
Education: Graduated from the Virginia Military Institute in 1849. Graduated from the University of Virginia in 1850.
Brigadier General: November 14, 1864, to rank from November 1, 1864.
Died: March 29, 1904, in Washington, D.C.
Buried: Warrenton, Virginia in the City Cemetery.

William Raine Peck
Born: January 31, 1818, in Jefferson County, Tennessee.
Brigadier General: February 22, 1865, to rank from February 18, 1865.
Died: January 22, 1871, at his plantation in Jefferson County, Tennessee.
Buried: Westview Cemetery in Jefferson City, Tennessee.

John Pegram
Born: January 24, 1832, in Petersburg, Virginia.
Education: Graduated from West Point in 1854. He ranked 10th in his class of 46.
Brigadier General: November 10, 1862, to rank from November 7, 1862.
Died: February 6, 1865, during the Battle of Hatcher's Run.
Buried: Hollywood Cemetery in Richmond, Virginia.

William Dorsey Pender
Born: February 6, 1834, in Edgecomb County, North Carolina.
Education: Graduated from West Point in 1854. He ranked 19th in a class of 46.
Brigadier General: July 22, 1862, to rank from June 3, 1862.
Major General: May 27, 1863, to rank from the same date.
Died: July 18, 1863, in Staunton, Virginia.
Buried: Tarboro, North Carolina in the yard of the Calvary Church.

William Nelson Pendleton
Born: December 26, 1809, in Richmond, Virginia.
Education: Graduated from West Point in 1830. He ranked fifth out of 42.
Brigadier General: March 26, 1862, to rank from the same date.
Died: January 15, 1883, in Lexington, Virginia.
Buried: Jackson Memorial Cemetery in Lexington, Virginia.

Abner Monroe Perrin
Born: February 2, 1827, in Edgefield District, South Carolina.
Brigadier General: September 17, 1862, to rank from September 10, 1862.
Died: May 12, 1864, during the Battle of Spotsylvania.
Buried: City Cemetery in Fredericksburg, Virginia.

Edward Aylesworth Perry
Born: March 15, 1831, in Richmond, Massachusetts.
Brigadier General: September 30, 1862, to rank from August 28, 1862.
Died: October 15, 1889, in Kerrville, Texas.
Buried: St. John's Cemetery in Pensacola, Florida.

William Flank Perry
Born: March 12, 1823, in Jackson County, Georgia.
Brigadier General: March 16, 1865, to rank from February 21, 1865.
Died: December 18, 1901, in Bowling Green, Kentucky.
Buried: Fairview Cemetery in Bowling Green, Kentucky.

James Johnston Pettigrew
Born: July 4, 1828, at "Bonarva" in Tyrell County, North Carolina.
Education: Attended the University of North Carolina.
Brigadier General: February 26, 1862, to rank from the same date.
Died: July 17, 1863, near Bunker Hill, North Carolina.
Buried: Pettigrew State Park in Tyrell County, North Carolina.

George Edward Pickett
Born: January 28, 1825, in Richmond, Virginia.
Education: Graduated from West Point in 1846. He ranked 59th out of 59.
Brigadier General: February 13, 1862, to rank from January 14, 1862.
Major General: October 11, 1862, to rank from October 10, 1862.
Died: July 30, 1875, in Norfolk, Virginia.
Buried: Hollywood Cemetery in Richmond, Virginia.

Carnot Posey
Born: August 5, 1818, in Wilkinson County, Mississippi.
Education: Attended the University of Virginia.
Brigadier General: November 1, 1862, to rank from the same date.
Died: November 13, 1863, at Charlottesville, Virginia.
Buried: University Cemetery at the University of Virginia in Charlottesville, Virginia.

Roger Atkinson Pryor
Born: July 19, 1828, near Petersburg, Virginia.
Education: Graduated from Hampden-Sydney College in 1845.
He also attended the University of Virginia.
Brigadier General: April 16, 1862, to rank from the same date.
Died: March 14, 1919, in New York City.
Buried: Princeton Cemetery in Princeton, New Jersey.

Gabriel James Rains
Born: June 4, 1803, in New Bern, North Carolina.
Education: Graduated from West Point in 1827. He ranked 13th in his class.
Brigadier General: September 23, 1861, to rank from the same date.
Died: August 6, 1881, in Aiken, South Carolina.
Buried: St. Thaddeus Cemetery in Aiken, South Carolina.

Stephen Dodson Ramseur
Born: May 31, 1837, in Lincolnton, North Carolina.
Education: Graduated from West Point in 1860. He ranked 14th in a
class of 41.
Brigadier General: November 1, 1862, to rank from the same date.
Major General: June 1, 1864, to rank from the same date.
Died: October 20, 1864, after being mortally wounded during the Battle
of Cedar Creek on October 19.
Buried: St. Luke's Church Cemetery in Lincolnton, North Carolina.

Matthew Whitaker Ransom
Born: October 8, 1826, in Warren County, North Carolina.
Education: Graduated from the University of North Carolina in 1847.
Brigadier General: June 15, 1863, to rank from June 13, 1863.
Died: October 8, 1904, near Garysburg, North Carolina.
Buried: On his plantation near Jackson, North Carolina.

Robert Ransom, Jr.
Born: February 12, 1828, in Warren County, North Carolina.
Education: Graduated from West Point in 1850. He ranked 18th out of 44.
Brigadier General: March 6, 1862, to rank from March 1, 1862.
Major General: May 26, 1863, to rank from May 25, 1863.
Died: January 14, 1892, at New Bern, North Carolina.
Buried: Cedar Grove Cemetery in New Bern, North Carolina.

Roswell Sabine Ripley
Born: March 14, 1823, at Worthington, Ohio.
Education: Graduated from West Point in 1843. He ranked seventh in a
class of 39.
Brigadier General: August 15, 1861, to rank from the same date.
Died: March 29, 1887, at the New York Hotel.
Buried: Magnolia Cemetery at Charleston, North Carolina.

William Paul Roberts
Born: July 11, 1841, in Gates County, North Carolina.
Brigadier General: February 23, 1865, to rank from February 21, 1865.
Died: March 28, 1910, at Norfolk, North Carolina.
Buried: Old City Cemetery in Gatesville, North Carolina.

Beverly Holcombe Robertson
Born: June 5, 1827, at "The Oaks" in Amelia County, Virginia.
Education: Graduated from West Point in 1849.
Brigadier General: June 9, 1862, to rank from the same date.
Died: November 12, 1910, in Washington, D.C.
Buried: Amelia County, Virginia.

Jerome Bonaparte Robertson
Born: March 14, 1815, in Woodford County, Kentucky.
Education: Graduated from Transylvania University in 1835.
Brigadier General: November 1, 1862, to rank from the same date.
Died: January 7, 1891, in Waco, Texas.
Buried: Oakwood Cemetery in Waco, Texas.

Robert Emmett Rodes
Born: March 29, 1829, at Lynchburg, Virginia.
Education: Graduated from the Virginia Military Institute in 1848.
Brigadier General: October 21, 1861, to rank from the same date.
Major General: May 7, 1863, to rank from May 2, 1863.
Died: September 19, 1864, in Winchester, Virginia.
Buried: Presbyterian Cemetery in Lynchburg, Virginia.

Thomas Lafayette Rosser
Born: October 15, 1836, in Campbell County, Virginia.
Education: Attended West Point but did not graduate.
Brigadier General: October 10, 1863, to rank from September 28, 1863.
Major General: November 4, 1864, to rank from the same date.
Died: March 29, 1910, in Charlottesville, Virginia.
Buried: Riverview Cemetery in Charlottesville, Virginia.

John Caldwell Calhoun Sanders
Born: April 4, 1840, at Tuscaloosa, Alabama.
Education: Graduated from State University in 1858.
Brigadier General: June 4, 1864, to rank from May 31, 1864.
Died: August 21, 1864, at the battle of Globe Tavern, Virginia.
Buried: Hollywood Cemetery in Richmond, Virginia.

Alfred Moore Scales

Born: November 26, 1827, at Reidsville, North Carolina.
Education: Attended State University.
Brigadier General: June 15, 1863, to rank from June 13, 1863.
Died: February 8, 1892, at Greensboro, North Carolina.
Buried: Green Hill Cemetery in Greensboro, North Carolina.

Paul Jones Semmes

Born: June 4, 1815, at Montford's Plantation, Wilkes County, Georgia.
Education: Attended the University of Virginia.
Brigadier General: March 18, 1862, to rank from March 11, 1862.
Died: July 9, 1863, from a mortal wound received on July 2, 1863.
Buried: Linnwood Cemetery in Columbus, Georgia.

James Phillip Simms

Born: January 16, 1837, in Covington, Georgia.
Brigadier General: February 18, 1865, to rank from December 8, 1864.
Died: May 30, 1887, at Covington, Georgia.
Buried: City Cemetery in Covington, Georgia.

Gustavus Woodson Smith

Born: November 30 or December 1, 1821, in Georgetown, Kentucky.
Education: Graduated from West Point in 1842. He ranked 8th out of 56.
Major General: September 19, 1861, to rank from the same date.
Died: June 24, 1896, at New York City.
Buried: Cedar Grove Cemetery in New London, Connecticut.

William Smith

Born: September 6, 1797, in King George County, Virginia.
Brigadier General: April 23, 1863, to rank from January 31, 1863.
Major General: August 13, 1863, to rank from August 12, 1863.
Died: May 18, 1887, near Warrenton, Virginia.
Buried: Hollywood Cemetery in Richmond, Virginia.

Gilbert Moxley Sorrel

Born: February 23, 1838, at Savannah, Georgia.
Brigadier General: October 31, 1864, to rank from October 27, 1864.
Died: August 10, 1901, near Roanoke, Virginia.
Buried: Laurel Grove Cemetery in Savannah, Georgia.

Leroy Augustus Stafford

Born: April 13, 1822, at "Greenwood" near Cheneyville, Louisiana.
Brigadier General: October 8, 1863, to rank from the same date.
Died: May 8, 1864, at Richmond, Virginia from a wound received on May
    5, 1864, at the Battle of the Wilderness.
Buried: Greenwood Plantation in Cheneyville, Louisiana.

William Edwin Starke
Born: 1814 in Brunswick County, Virginia.
Brigadier General: August 6, 1862, to rank from the same date.
Died: September 17, 1862, after being hit by three minie balls during the Battle of Antietam.
Buried: Hollywood Cemetery in Richmond, Virginia.

Walter Husted Stevens
Born: August 24, 1827, in Penn Yan, New York.
Education: Graduated from West Point in 1848. He ranked fourth in the class.
Brigadier General: September 2, 1864, to rank from August 28, 1864.
Died: November 12, 1867, in Veracruz, Mexico.
Buried: Hollywood Cemetery in Richmond, Virginia.

George Hume Steuart
Born: August 24, 1828, in Baltimore, Maryland.
Education: Graduated from West Point in 1848. He ranked 37th in a class of 38.
Brigadier General: March 18, 1862, to rank from March 6, 1862.
Died: November 22, 1903, in South River, Maryland.
Buried: Green Mount Cemetery in Baltimore, Maryland.

James Ewell Brown Stuart
Born: February 6, 1833, in Patrick County, Virginia.
Education: Graduated from West Point in 1854. He ranked 13th in the class.
Brigadier General: September 24, 1861, to rank from the same date.
Major General: July 25, 1862, to rank from the same date.
Died: May 12, 1864, after being mortally wounded on May 11, 1864, at the Battle of Yellow Tavern.
Buried: Hollywood Cemetery in Richmond, Virginia.

William Booth Taliaferro
Born: December 28, 1822, at "Belleville" in Gloucester County, Virginia.
Education: Graduated from William and Mary College in 1841. Also attended Harvard University.
Brigadier General: March 6, 1862, to rank from March 4, 1862.
Died: February 27, 1898, in Gloucester County, Virginia.
Buried: Ware Church Cemetery in Gloucester County, Virginia.

James Barbour Terrill
Born: February 20, 1838, at "Warm Springs" in Bath County, Virginia.
Education: Graduated from the Virginia Military Institute in 1858.
Brigadier General: May 31, 1864, to rank from the same date.
Died: May 30, 1864, in an encounter at Bethesda Church, Virginia.
Buried: Bethesda Church on the battlefield by Federal troops.

William Richard Terry
Born: March 12, 1827, in Liberty, Virginia.
Education: Graduated from the Virginia Military Institute in 1850. Also attended the University of Virginia.
Brigadier General: June 10, 1864, to rank from May 31, 1864.
Died: March 28, 1897, in Chesterfield Court House, Virginia.
Buried: Hollywood Cemetery in Richmond, Virginia.

Edward Lloyd Thomas
Born: March 23, 1825, in Clarke County, Georgia.
Brigadier General: November 1, 1862, to rank from the same date.
Died: March 8, 1898, in South McAlester, Indian Territory.
Buried: Kiowa, Oklahoma.

Robert Augustus Toombs
Born: July 2, 1810, in Wilkes County, Georgia.
Education: Graduated from Union College in 1828.
Brigadier General: July 19, 1861, to rank from the same date.
Died: December 15, 1885, in Washington, Georgia.
Buried: Rest Haven Cemetery in Washington, Georgia.

Thomas Fentress Toon
Born: June 10, 1840, in Columbus County, North Carolina.
Brigadier General: May 31, 1864, to rank from the same date.
Died: February 19, 1902, in Raleigh, North Carolina.
Buried: Oakwood Cemetery in Raleigh, North Carolina.

Isaac Ridgeway Trimble
Born: May 15, 1802, in Culpeper County, Virginia.
Education: Graduated from West Point in 1822. He ranked 17th out of a class of 42.
Brigadier General: August 9, 1861, to rank from the same date.
Major General: January 17, 1863, to rank from the same date.
Died: January 2, 1888, in Baltimore, Maryland.
Buried: Green Mount Cemetery in Baltimore, Maryland.

Henry Harrison Walker
Born: October 15, 1832, at "Elmwood" in Sussex County, Virginia.
Education: Graduated from West Point in 1853. He ranked 41st in a class of 52.
Brigadier General: July 1, 1863, to rank from the same date.
Died: March 22, 1912, at Morristown, New Jersey.
Buried: Evergreen Cemetery in Morristown, New Jersey.

James Alexander Walker
Born: August 27, 1832, in Augusta County, Virginia.
Brigadier General: May 16, 1863, to rank from May 15, 1863.
Died: October 20, 1901, in Wytheville, Virginia.
Buried: City Cemetery in Wytheville, Virginia.

John George Walker
Born: July 22, 1822, in Cole County, Missouri.
Brigadier General: January 9, 1862, to rank from the same date.
Major General: November 8, 1862, to rank from the same date.
Died: July 20, 1893, in Washington, D.C.
Buried: Mount Hebron Cemetery in Winchester, Virginia.

Reuben Lindsay Walker
Born: May 29, 1827, in Logan, Virginia.
Brigadier General: February 18, 1865, to rank from the same date.
Died: June 7, 1890, in Fluvanna County, Virginia.
Buried: Hollywood Cemetery in Richmond, Virginia.

William Henry Wallace
Born: March 24, 1827, in Laurens District, South Carolina.
Brigadier General: September 20, 1864, to rank from the same date.
Died: March 21, 1901, in Union, South Carolina.
Buried: Presbyterian Cemetery in Union, South Carolina.

David Addison Weisiger
Born: December 23, 1818, at "The Grove" in Chesterfield County, Virginia.
Brigadier General: May 31, 1864, to rank from the same date.
Died: February 23, 1899, in Richmond, Virginia.
Buried: Blandford Cemetery in Petersburg, Virginia.

Gabriel Colvin Wharton
Born: July 23, 1824, in Culpeper County, Virginia.
Education: Graduated from the Virginia Military Institute in 1847.
Brigadier General: September 25, 1863, to rank from the same date.
Died: May 12, 1906, at Radford, Virginia.
Buried: Family cemetery in Radford, Virginia.

William Henry Chase Whiting
Born: March 22, 1824, in Biloxi, Mississippi.
Brigadier General: August 28, 1861, to rank from July 21, 1861.
Major General: April 22, 1863, to rank from February 28, 1863.
Died: March 10, 1865, at Fort Columbus, Governors Island, New York Harbor.
Buried: Oakdale Cemetery in Wilmington, North Carolina.

Williams Carter Wickham
Born: September 21, 1820, in Richmond, Virginia.
Brigadier General: September 2, 1863, to rank from September 1, 1863.
Died: July 23, 1888, in Richmond, Virginia.
Buried: Hickory Hill Cemetery in Hanover County, Virginia.

Cadmus Marcellus Wilcox
Born: May 29, 1824, in Wayne County, North Carolina.
Education: Graduated from West Point in 1846. He ranked 54th in a class of 59.
Brigadier General: October 21, 1861, to rank from the same date.
Major General: August 13, 1863, to rank from the same date.
Died: December 2, 1890, in Washington, D.C.
Buried: Oak Hill Cemetery in Washington, D.C.

Charles Sidney Winder
Born: October 18, 1829, in Talbot County, Maryland.
Education: Graduated from West Point in 1850. He ranked 22nd in a class of 45.
Brigadier General: March 7, 1862, to rank from March 1, 1862.
Died: August 9, 1862, at the Battle of Cedar Mountain, Virginia.
Buried: Lloyd Family Cemetery near Easton, Maryland.

Henry Alexander Wise
Born: December 3, 1806, in Drumondtown, Virginia.
Education: Graduated from Washington College in 1825.
Brigadier General: June 5, 1861, to rank from the same date.
Died: September 12, 1876, in Richmond, Virginia.
Buried: Hollywood Cemetery in Richmond, Virginia.

William Tatum Wofford
Born: June 28, 1824, in Habersham County, Georgia.
Brigadier General: April 23, 1863, to rank from January 17, 1863.
Died: May 22, 1884, near Cass Station, Georgia.
Buried: Cassville City Cemetery in Cassville, Georgia.

Ambrose Ransom Wright
Born: April 26, 1826, in Louisville, Georgia.
Brigadier General: June 3, 1862, to rank from the same date.
Major General: November 30, 1864, to rank from November 26, 1864.
Died: December 21, 1872, in Augusta, Georgia.
Buried: Magnolia Cemetery in Augusta, Georgia.

Zebulon York

Born: October 10, 1819, in Avon, Maine.
Education: Attended the University of Louisiana.
Brigadier General: May 31, 1864, to rank from the same date.
Died: August 5, 1900, in Natchez, Mississippi.
Buried: City Cemetery in Natchez, Mississippi.

Pierce Manning Butler Young

Born: November 15, 1836, in Spartanburg, North Carolina.
Brigadier General: September 28, 1863, to rank from the same date.
Died: July 6, 1896, in New York City.
Buried: Oak Hill Cemetery in Cartiersville, Georgia, on his plantation.

Bibliography

Alexander, Bevin. *Robert E. Lee's Civil War*. Holbrook, Mass.: Adams Media Corporation, 1998.

Axelrod, Alan. *The Complete Idiot's Guide to the Civil War*. New York: Alpha Books, 1998.

Bailey, Ronald H. *The Bloodiest Day: The Battle of Antietam*. Alexandria, Va.: Time-Life Books, Inc., 1984.

Boatner, Mark M. *The Civil War Dictionary*. New York: Random House, 1958.

Bowman, John S., ed. *The Civil War Almanac*. New York: World Almanac Publications, 1983.

Brown, Herbert O., and Dwight V. Nitz. *Fields of Glory: The Fact Book of the Battle of Gettysburg*. Gettysburg, Pa.: Thomas Publications, 1990.

Buell, Thomas B. *The Warrior Generals: Combat Leadership in the Civil War*. New York: Crown Publishers, Inc., 1997.

Davis, William C. *Battle at Bull Run*. Baton Rouge: Louisiana State University Press, 1977.

Davis, William C., ed. *The Confederate Generals*. 6 volumes. The National Historical Society, 1991.

Davis, William C. *Rebels & Yankees: The Colanders of the Civil War*. New York: Gallery Books, 1990.

Dowdey, Clifford. *Death of a Nation: The Story of Lee and His Men At Gettysburg*. New York: Alfred A. Knopf, 1958.

————. *The History of the Confederacy, 1832–1865*. New York: Barnes & Noble Books, 1992.

————. *The Seven Days: The Emergence Of Lee*. Boston: Little, Brown, 1964.

Faust, Patricia L., ed. *Historical Times Illustrated Encyclopedia of the Civil War*. New York: Harper & Row, 1986.

Freeman, Douglas Southall. *Lee's Lieutenants*. 3 volumes. New York: Charles Scribner's Sons, 1942–1944.

Furgurson, Ernest B. *Chancellorsville, 1863: The Souls of the Brave*. New York: Alfred A. Knopf, 1992.

Gallagher, Gary W. *Stephen Dodson Ramseur: Lee's Gallant General*. Chapel Hill: University of North Carolina Press, 1985.

Garrison, Webb. *Civil War Stories: Strange Tales, Oddities, Events & Coincidences*. New York: Promontory Press, 1997.

———. *Civil War Trivia and Fact Book*. Nashville, Tenn.: Rutledge Hill Press, 1992.

Hattaway, Herman, and Archer Jones. *How the North Won: A Military History of the Civil War*. Urbana: University of Illinois Press, 1983.

Hennessy, John J. *The Return to Bull Run: The Campaign and Battle of Second Manassas*. New York: Simon & Schuster, 1993.

Hightower, John M. *The Confederate Challenge*. Natural Bridge Station, Va.: Rockbridge Publishing Company, 1992.

Lang, J. Stephen. *The Complete Book of Confederate Trivia*. Shippensburg, Pa.: Burd Street Press, 1996.

Leckie, Robert. *None Died in Vain*. New York: Harper Collins Publishers, 1990.

Lewis, Thomas A. *The Shenandoah In Flames: The Valley Campaign of 1864*. Alexandria, Va.: Time-Life Books, 1987.

Martin, Samuel J. *The Road to Glory: Confederate General Richard S. Ewell*. Indianapolis, Ind.: Guild Press of Indiana, Inc., 1991.

Matter, William D. *If It Takes All Summer: The Battle of Spotsylvania*. Chapel Hill: The University of North Carolina Press, 1988.

McMurry, Richard M. *John Bell Hood and the War For Southern Independence*. Lincoln: University of Nebraska Press, 1982.

Motts, Wayne E. *"Trust in God and Fear Nothing": Gen. Lewis A. Armistead, CSA*. Gettysburg, Pa.: Farnsworth House Military Impressions, 1994.

Osborne, Charles C. *Jubal: The Life and Times of General Jubal A. Early, CSA, Defender of the Lost Cause*. Chapel Hill: Algonquin Books of Chapel Hill, 1992.

Pfanz, Donald C. *Richard S. Ewell: A Soldier's Life*. Chapel Hill: The University of North Carolina Press, 1998.

Pollard, Edward A. *Lee and His Lieutenants*. New York: E.B. Treat & Co., 1867.

Rawls, Walton, ed. *Great Civil War Heroes and Their Battles*. New York: Abbeville Press, 1985.

Rhea, Gordon C. *The Battle of the Wilderness, May 5-6, 1864*. Baton Rouge: Louisiana State University Press, 1994.

Robertson, James I., Jr. *Civil War Virginia: Battleground For a Nation*. Charlottesville: University Press of Virginia, 1991.

———. *General A.P. Hill: The Story of a Confederate Warrior*. New York: Random House, 1987.

———. *Stonewall Jackson: The Man, The Soldier, The Legend*. New York: Macmillan Publishing, 1997.

Sears, Stephen W. *Chancellorsville*. Boston: Houghton Mifflin Company, 1996.
———. *Landscape Turned Red: The Battle of Antietam*. Boston: Houghton Mifflin Company, 1983.
Selcer, Richard F. *"Faithfully and Forever Your Soldier": Gen. George E. Pickett, CSA*. Gettysburg, Pa.: Farnsworth House Military Impressions, 1995.
Sifakis, Stewart. *Who Was Who in the Confederacy*. New York: Facts on File, 1988.
Tagg, Larry. *The Generals of Gettysburg*. Campbell, Calif.: Savas Publishing Company, 1998.
Thomas, Emory M. *Bold Dragoon: The Life of J.E.B. Stuart*. New York: Harper & Row, Publishers, 1986.
Thomason, John. *Jeb Stuart*. New York: Charles Scribner's Sons, 1930.
Tucker, Glenn. *High Tide at Gettysburg: The Campaign in Pennsylvania*. Gettysburg, Pa.: Stan Clark Military Books, 1995.
Warner, Ezra J. *Generals in Gray*. Baton Rouge: Louisiana State University Press, 1959.
Welsh, Jack D., MD. *Medical Histories of Confederate Generals*. Kent, Ohio: Kent State University Press, 1995.
Wert, Jeffry D. *From Winchester to Cedar Creek: the Shenandoah Campaign of 1864*. New York: Simon & Schuster, 1987.
———. *General James Longstreet: the Confederacy's Most Controversial Soldier—A Biography*. New York: Simon & Schuster, 1993.
Wheeler, Richard. *Lee's Terrible Swift Sword: From Antietam to Chancellorsville An Eyewitness History*. New York: Harper Collins Publishers, 1992.

The Gray Riders

Stories from the Confederate Cavalry

Compiled by Lee Jacobs

What was it like to ride with Stuart, Forrest, or Mosby? Here are stories from the Confederate cavalry, expressing the experiences and emotions of those who served as the "eyes and ears" of the army. Some tales are humorous; others portray comradeship, pride, and patriotism.

Unlike the large-scale artillery and infantry battles, most cavalry fights were skirmishes among small groups of mounted men, often serving as scouts. "They fell not by scores and hundreds, but by two and tens." Even their enemies spoke of the Confederate cavalry with admiration.

Lee Jacobs has brought units like the Terry Texas Rangers and individuals to life in this collection of deeply felt experiences of horse soldiers in both east and west.

LEE JACOBS is the great-grandson of a Confederate cavalryman. Over the years he has had the opportunity to travel from Virginia to Texas. During this time, he completed much of his research for this book. He has visited battlefields, historic sites, libraries, and archives to verify facts.

ISBN 1-57249-153-1 • LC 98-47398 • 6 x 9 • 204 Pages • Bibliography • Index • SC $19.95

Confederate Letters and Diaries 1861-1865

Edited by Walbrook D. Swank

Confederate Letters and Diaries brings to modern readers many interesting, fascinating writings of Confederate soldiers. Colonel Swank has included numerous eyewitness, and often heart rending accounts of battlefield scenes, hardships faced in camp, on the march, or in prison—this collection even includes a diary of a Virginia cavalryman held in a Federal military prison. The words of those soldiers from Dixie bring their turbulent years strikingly alive.

Following many years of distinguished service in the United States Air Force, which included a short tour of duty in the White House, COLONEL WALBROOK D. SWANK has produced this unique book.

ISBN 0-942597-25-7 • $5^1/_2$ x $8^1/_2$ • 200 Pages • SC $17.95

The CSS *H. L. Hunley*
Confederate Submarine
R. Thomas Campbell

Visible from the waterfront and the "battery" almost every evening during the approaching winter of 1863 was the long, low shape of a peculiar-looking vessel. Its unique position rested with a blackened iron hull barely awash in the rippling harbor waters. Usually near sundown, observers would notice nine men, two of them officers, clamber onto the craft and disappear into its interior. A tall sailor, standing in an open hatchway, would cast off the lines and then he, too, would vanish below.

In spite of several failures, little did the residents of the city realize that they were historic witnesses to what would become the world's first successful submarine. Forerunner of all the great and fearsome undersea craft to come in a later century, this historic vessel that they were watching was the Confederate submarine, CSS *H. L. Hunley*. No other vessel built by or for the Confederacy is as intriguing and innovative as the *Hunley*. Even the swift cruisers such as the *Alabama* or *Shenandoah* or the mighty ironclads like *Virginia*, *Arkansas* or *Tennessee* cannot rival the little *Hunley* for its sheer genius in concept, construction, and operation. The Southern volunteers who crewed this small submarine, and lost their lives in doing so, were entering a realm that few in the nineteenth century could conceive or understand. It required extraordinary courage to enter this realm. On at least two occasions, when the *Hunley* was lost and the crew suffocated, Confederate Navy volunteers had stepped forward to form a new crew even before the craft was salvaged from the ocean floor. They knew only too well that if the sub ran into trouble while submerged that there was no way to replenish the air supply. They could do little but await the inevitable end.

This is the story of those dedicated men and the fascinating machine they took into battle.

R. THOMAS CAMPBELL is a graduate of the Wharton School of Business and Finance at the University of Pennsylvania, and holds a Bachelor of Science degree from Villanova University. He is currently preparing additional studies of the activities of the Confederate Navy.

NOW A TELEVISION MOVIE

ISBN 1-57249-175-2 • LC 99-35335 • 6 x 9 • 185 Pages • 60 Illustrations • Bibliography • Index • SC $14.95